THE ETHICS OF THE DUST.

SPHYNX AND PYRAMID.

THE

ETHICS OF THE DUST

Ten Lectures

TO

LITTLE HOUSEWIVES

ON

The Elements of Crystallization.

BY

JOHN RUSKIN, LL.D.,

Honorary Student of Christ Church, and Slade Professor of Fine Atr.

———————

NEW YORK:
METROPOLITAN PUBLISHING CO.

CONTENTS.

————

PERSONÆ.

LECTURE 1.

THE VALLEY OF DIAMONDS.

THE ETHICS OF THE DUST.

LECTURE I.

THE VALLEY OF DIAMONDS.

A very idle talk, by the dining-room fire, after raisin-and-almond time.

OLD LECTURER; FLORRIE, ISABEL, MAY, LILY, *and* SIBYL.

OLD LECTURER (L.). Come here, Isabel, and tell me what the make-believe was, this afternoon.

ISABEL (*arranging herself very primly on the foot-stool*). Such a dreadful one ! Florrie and I were lost in the Valley of Diamonds.

L. What ! Sindbad's, which nobody could get out of?

ISABEL. Yes ; but Florrie and I got out of it.

L. So I see. At least, I see you did; but are you sure Florrie did ?

ISABEL. Quite sure.

FLORRIE (*putting her head round from be-*

hind L.'s *sofa-cushion*).   Quite sure.   (*Disappears again.*)

L. I think I could be made to feel surer about it.

(FLORRIE *reappears, gives* L. *a kiss, and again exit.*)

L. I suppose it's all right; but how did you manage it?

ISABEL. Well, you know, the eagle that took up Sindbad was very large—very, very large—the largest of all the eagles.

L. How large were the others?

ISABEL. I don't quite know—they were so far off.   But this one was, oh, so big! and it had great wings, as wide as—twice over the ceiling.   So, when it was picking up Sindbad, Florrie and I thought it wouldn't know if we got on its back too: so I got up first, and then I pulled up Florrie, and we put our arms round its neck, and away it flew.

L. But why did you want to get out of the valley? and why haven't you brought me some diamonds?

ISABEL. It was because of the serpents.   I couldn't pick up even the least little bit of a diamond, I was so frightened.

L. You should not have minded the serpents.

ISABEL. Oh, but suppose that they had minded me?

L. We all of us mind you a little too much, Isabel, I'm afraid.

ISABEL No—no—no, indeed.

L. I tell you what, Isabel—I don't believe either Sindbad, or Florrie, or you, ever were in the Valley of Diamonds.

ISABEL. You naughty ! when I tell you we were !

L. Because you say you were frightened at the serpents.

ISABEL. And wouldn't you have been ?

L. Not at those serpents. Nobody who really goes into the valley is ever frightened at them—they are so beautiful.

ISABEL (*suddenly serious*). But there's no real Valley of Diamonds, is there ?

L. Yes, Isabel ; very real indeed.

FLORRIE (*reappearing*). Oh, where? Tell me about it.

L. I cannot tell you a great deal about it ; only I know it is very different from Sindbad's. In his valley, there was only a diamond lying here and there ; but, in the real valley, there are diamonds covering the grass in showers every morning, instead of dew : and there are clusters of trees, which look like lilac-trees ; but, in spring, all their blossoms are of amethyst.

FLORRIE. But there can't be any serpents there, then ?

L. Why not ?

FLORRIE. Because they don't come into such beautiful places.

L. I never said it was a beautiful place.

FLORRIE. What ! not with diamonds strewed about it like dew ?

L. That's according to your fancy, Florrie. For myself, I like dew better.

Isabel. Oh, but the dew won't stay; it all dries!

L. Yes; and it would be much nicer if the diamonds dried too, for the people in the valley have to sweep them off the grass, in heaps, whenever they want to walk on it; and then the heaps glitter so, they hurt one's eyes.

Florrie. Now you're just playing, you know.

L. So are you, you know.

Florrie. Yes, but you mustn't play.

L. That's very hard, Florrie; why mustn't I, if you may?

Florrie. Oh, I may, because I'm little, but you mustn't, because you're—(*hesitates for a delicate expression of magnitude*).

L. (*rudely taking the first that comes*). Because I'm big? No; that's not the way of it at all, Florrie. Because you're little, you should have very little play; and because I'm big I should have a great deal.

Isabel *and* Florrie (*both*). No—no—no —no. That isn't it at all. (Isabel *sola, quoting Miss Ingelow.*) "The lambs play always —they know no better." (*Putting her head very much on one side.*) Ah, now—please —please—tell us true; we want to know.

L. But why do you want me to tell you true, any more than the man who wrote the "Arabian Nights"?

ISABEL. Because—because we like to know about real things ; and you can tell us, and we can't ask the man who wrote the stories.

L. What do you call real things ?

ISABEL. Now, you know ! Things that really are.

L. Whether you can see them or not ?

ISABEL. Yes, if somebody else saw them.

L. But if nobody has ever seen them ?

ISABEL (*evading the point*). Well, but, you know, if there were a real Valley of Diamonds, somebody *must* have seen it.

L. You cannot be so sure of that, Isabel. Many people go to real places, and never see them ; and many people pass through this valley, and never see it.

FLORRIE. What stupid people they must be !

L. No, Florrie. They are much wiser than the people who do see it.

MAY. I think I know where it is.

ISABEL. Tell us more about it, and then we'll guess.

L. Well. There's a great broad road, by a river-side, leading up into it.

MAY (*gravely cunning, with emphasis on the last word*). Does the road really go *up* ?

L. You think it should go down into a valley ? No, it goes up ; this is a valley among the hills, and it is as high as the clouds, and is often full of them ; so that even the people who most want to see it, cannot, always.

ISABEL. And what is the river beside the road like?

L. It ought to be very beautiful because it flows over diamond sand—only the water is thick and red.

ISABEL. Red water?

L. It isn't all water.

MAY. Oh, please never mind that, Isabel, just now; I want to hear about the valley.

L. So the entrance to it is very wide, under a steep rock; only such numbers of people are always trying to get in, that they keep jostling each other, and manage it but slowly. Some weak ones are pushed back, and never get in at all; and make great moaning as they go away: but perhaps they are none the worse in the end.

MAY. And when one gets in, what is it like?

L. It is up and down, broken kind of ground : the road stops directly ; and there are great dark rocks, covered all over with wild gourds and wild vines; the gourds, if you cut them, are red, with black seeds, like watermelons, and look ever so nice ; and the people of the place make a red pottage of them : but you must take care not to eat any if you ever want to leave the valley (though I believe putting plenty of meal in it makes it wholesome). Then the wild vines have clusters of the color of amber; and the people of the country say they are the grape of Eshcol; and sweeter than

honey : but, indeed, if anybody else tastes
them, they are like gall. Then there are
thickets of bramble, so thorny that they
would be cut away directly, anywhere else;
but here they are covered with little cinque-
foiled blossoms of pure silver ; and, for
berries, they have clusters of rubies. Dark
rubies, which you only see are red after
gathering them. But you may fancy what
blackberry parties the children have ! Only
they get their frocks and hands sadly torn.

LILY. But rubies can't spot one's frocks,
as blackberries do ?

L. No ; but I'll tell you what spots them
—the mulberries. There are great forests
of them, all up the hills, covered with silk-
worms, some munching the leaves so loud
that it is like mills at work ; and some
spinning. But the berries are the blackest
you ever saw ; and, wherever they fall, they
stain a deep red ; and nothing ever washes
it out again. And it is their juice, soaking
through the grass, which makes the river so
red, because all its springs are in this wood.
And the boughs of the trees are twisted, as
if in pain, like old olive branches ; and their
leaves are dark. And it is in these forests
that the serpents are ; but nobody is afraid
of them. They have fine crimson crests,
and they are wreathed about the wild
branches, one in every tree, nearly ; and
they are singing serpents, for the serpents
are, in this forest, what birds are in ours.

FLORRIE. Oh, I don't want to go there at all, now.

L. You would like it very much indeed, Florrie, if you were there. The serpents would not bite you; the only fear would be of your turning into one!

FLORRIE. Oh, dear, but that's worse.

L. You wouldn't think so if you really were turned into one, Florrie; you would be very proud of your crest. And as long as you were yourself (not that you could get there if you remained quite the little Florrie you are now), you would like to hear the serpents sing. They hiss a little through it, like the cicadas in Italy; but they keep good time, and sing delightful melodies; and most of them have seven heads, with throats which each take a note of the octave; so that they can sing chords—it is very fine indeed. And the fireflies fly round the edge of the forest all the night long; you wade in fireflies, they make the fields look like a lake trembling with reflection of stars; but you must take care not to touch them, for they are not like Italian fireflies, but burn, like real sparks.

FLORRIE. I don't like it at all; I'll never go there.

L. I hope not, Florrie; or at least that you will get out again if you do. And it is very difficult to get out, for beyond these serpent forests there are great cliffs of dead gold, which form a labyrinth, winding

always higher and higher, till the gold is all
split asunder by wedges of ice ; and glaciers, welded, half of ice seven times frozen,
and half of gold seven times frozen, hang
down from them, and fall in thunder, cleaving
into deadly splinters, like the Cretan· arrow-
heads ; and into a mixed dust of snow and
gold, ponderous, yet which the mountain
whirlwinds are able to lift and drive in
wreaths and pillars, hiding the paths with a
burial cloud, fatal at once with wintry chill,
and weight of golden ashes. So the wan-
derers in the labyrinth fall, one by one, and
are buried there :—yet, over the drifted
graves, those who are spared climb to the
last, through coil on coil of the path ;—for
at the end of it they see the king of the valley, sitting on his throne : and beside him
(but it is only a false vision), spectra of creatures like themselves, sit on thrones, from
which they seem to look down on all the
kingdoms of the world, and the glory of
them.   And on the canopy of his throne
there is an inscription in fiery letters, which
they strive to read, but cannot ; for it is
written in words which are like the words
of all languages, and yet are of none.   Men
say it is more like their own tongue to the
English than it is to any other nation ; but
the only record of it is by an Italian, who
heard the king himself cry it as a war-cry,
" Pape Satan, Pape Satan Aleppe." *

* Dante, Inf. 7 1.

2

SIBYL. But do they all perish there? You said there was a way through the valley, and out of it.

L. Yes; but few find it. If any of them keep to the grass paths, where the diamonds are swept aside, and hold their hands over their eyes so as not to be dazzled, the grass paths lead forward gradually to a place where one sees a little opening in the golden rocks. You were at Chamouni last year, Sibyl; did your guide chance to show you the pierced rock of the Aiguille du Midi?

SIBYL. No, indeed, we only got up from Geneva on Monday night; and it rained all Tuesday; and we had to be back at Geneva again, early on Wednesday morning.

L. Of course. That is the way to see a country in a Sibylline manner, by inner consciousness: but you might have seen the pierced rock in your drive up, or down, if the clouds broke: not that there is much to see in it; one of the crags of the aiguille-edge, on the southern slope of it, is struck sharply through, as by an awl, into a little eyelet hole; which you may see, seven thousand feet above the valley (as the clouds flit past behind it, or leave the sky), first white, and then dark blue. Well, there's just such an eyelet hole in one of the upper crags of the Diamond Valley; and, from a distance, you think that it is no bigger than the eye of a needle. But if you get up to it, they say you may drive a loaded camel through it, and that there are fine things on the other side, but I have never spoken with anybody who had been through.

SIBYL. I think we understand it now. We will try to write it down, and think of it.

L. Meantime, Florrie, though all that I have been telling you is very true, yet you must not think the sort of diamonds that people wear in rings and necklaces are found lying about on the grass. Would you like to see how they really are found?

FLORRIE. Oh, yes—yes.

L. Isabel—or Lily—run up to my room and fetch me the little box with a glass lid out of the top drawer of the chest of drawers. (*Race between* LILY *and* ISABEL.)

(*Re-enter* ISABEL *with the box, very much out of breath.* LILY *behind.*)

L. Why, you never can beat Lily in a race on the stairs, can you, Isabel?

ISABEL (*panting*). Lily—beat me—ever so far—but she gave me—the box—to carry in.

L. Take off the lid, then; gently.

FLORRIE (*after peeping in, disappointed*). There's only a great ugly brown stone!

L. Not much more than that, certainly, Florrie, if people were wise. But look, it is not a single stone; but a knot of pebbles fastened together by gravel: and in the gravel, or compressed sand, if you look close you will see grains of gold glittering everywhere, all through; and then, do you see these two white beads, which shine, as if they had been covered with grease?

FLORRIE. May I touch them?

L. Yes; you will find they are not greasy, only very smooth. Well, those are the fatal jewels; native here in their dust with gold, so that you may see, cradled here together, the two great enemies of mankind,—the strongest of all malignant physical powers that have tormented our race.

SIBYL. Is that really so? I know they do great harm; but do they not also do great good?

L. My dear child, what good? Was any woman, do you suppose, ever the better for possessing diamonds? but how many have been made base, frivolous, and miserable by desiring them? Was ever man the better for having coffers full of gold? but who shall measure the guilt that is incurred to fill them? Look into the history of any civilized nations; analyze, with reference to this one cause of crime and misery, the lives and thoughts of their nobles, priests, merchants, and men of luxurious life. Every other temptation is at last concentrated into this: pride, and lust, and envy, and anger all give up their strength to avarice. The sin of the whole world is essentially the sin of Judas. Men do not disbelieve their Christ; but they sell Him.

SIBYL. But surely that is the fault of human nature? it is not caused by the accident, as

it were, of there being a pretty metal, like
gold, to be found by digging. If people
could not find that, would they not find
something else, and quarrel for it instead?

L. No. Wherever legislators have suc-
ceeded in excluding, for a time, jewels and
precious metals from among national possessions, the national spirit has remained
healthy. Covetousness is not natural to man
—generosity is; but covetousness must be
excited by a special cause, as a given disease
by a given miasma; and the essential nature
of a material for the excitement of covetousness is, that it shall be a beautiful thing
which can be retained *without a use.* The
moment we can use our possessions to any
good purpose ourselves, the instinct of com-
municating that use to others rises side by
side with our power. If you can read a
book rightly, you will want others to hear
it; if you can enjoy a picture rightly, you
will want others to see it: learn how to
manage a horse, a plough, or a ship, and
you will desire to make your subordinates
good horsemen, ploughmen, or sailors; you
will never be able to see the fine instrument
you are master of abused; but once fix
your desire on anything useless, and all the
purest pride and folly in your heart will mix
with the desire, and make you at last wholly
inhuman, a mere ugly lump of stomach and
suckers, like a cuttle-fish.

SIBYL. But surely, these two beautiful

things, gold and diamonds, must have been appointed to some good purpose?

L. Quite conceivably so, my dear: as also earthquakes and pestilences; but of such ultimate purposes we can have no sight. The practical, immediate office of the earthquake and pestilence is to slay us, like moths; and, as moths, we shall be wise to live out of their way. So, the practical, immediate office of gold and diamonds is the multiplied destruction of souls (in whatever sense you have been taught to understand that phrase); and the paralysis of wholesome human effort and thought on the face of God's earth: and a wise nation will live out of the way of them. The money which the English habitually spend in cutting diamonds would, in ten years, if it were applied to cutting rocks instead, leave no dangerous reef nor difficult harbor round the whole island coast. Great Britain would be a diamond worth cutting, indeed, a true piece of regalia. (*Leaves this to their thoughts for a little while*). Then, also, we poor mineralogists might sometimes have the chance of seeing a fine crystal of diamond unhacked by the jeweler.

SIBYL. Would it be more beautiful uncut?

L. No; but of infinite interest. We might even come to know something about the making of diamonds.

SIBYL. I thought the chemists could make them already?

L. In very small black crystals, yes; but no one knows how they are formed where they are found; or if indeed they are formed there at all. These, in my hand, look as if they had been swept down with the gravel and gold; only we can trace the gravel and gold to their native rocks, but not the diamonds. Read the account given of the diamond in any good work on mineralogy;— you will find nothing but lists of localities of gravel, or conglomerate rock (which is only an old indurated gravel). Some say it was once a vegetable gum; but it may have been charred wood; but what one would like to know is, mainly, why charcoal should make itself into diamonds in India, and only into black lead in Borrowdale.

SIBYL. Are they wholly the same, then?

L. There is a little iron mixed with our black lead; but nothing to hinder its crystallization. Your pencils in fact are all pointed with formless diamond, though they would be H H H pencils to purpose, if it crystallized.

SIBYL. But what *is* crystallization?

L. A pleasant question, when one's half asleep, and it has been tea-time these two hours. What thoughtless things girls are!

SIBYL. Yes, we are; but we want to know, for all that.

L. My dear, it would take a week to tell you.

SIBYL. Well, take it, and tell us.

L. But nobody knows anything about it.

Sibyl. Then tell us something that nobody knows.

L. Get along with you, and tell Dora to make tea.

> (*The house rises ; but of course the* Lec-
> turer *wanted to be forced to lecture
> again, and was.*)

LECTURE 2.

THE PYRAMID BUILDERS.

LECTURE II.

THE PYRAMID BUILDERS.

In the large Schoolroom, to which everybody has been summoned by ringing of the great bell.

L. So you have all actually come to hear about crystallization ! I cannot conceive why, unless the little ones think that the discussion may involve some reference to sugar-candy.

(*Symptoms of high displeasure among the younge memberrs of council.* ISA-BEL *frowns severely at* L., *and shakes her head violently.*)

My dear children, if you knew it, you are yourselves, at this moment, as you sit in your ranks, nothing, in the eye of a mineralogist, but a lovely group of rosy sugar-candy, arranged by atomic forces. And even admitting you to be something more, you have certainly been crystallizing without knowing it. Did not I hear a great hurrying and whispering, ten minutes ago, when you were late in from the playground; and thought you would not all be quietly seated by the time I was

27

ready :—besides some discussion about places—something about " it's not being fair that the little ones should always be nearest ? " Well, you were then all being crystallized. When you ran in from the garden, and against one another in the passages, you were in what mineralogists would call a state of solution, and gradual confluence ; when you got seated in those orderly rows, each in her proper place, you became crystalline. That is just what the atoms of a mineral do, if they can, whenever they get disordered : they get into order again as soon as may be.

I hope you feel inclined to interrupt me, and say, " But we know our places ; how do the atoms know theirs ? And sometimes we dispute about our places ; do the atoms —(and, besides, we don't like being compared to atoms at all)—never dispute about theirs ? " Two wise questions these, if you had a mind to put them ! it was long before I asked them myself, of myself. And I will not call you atoms any more. May I call you—let me see—" primary molecules " ? (*General dissent indicated in subdued but decisive murmurs.*) No ! not even, in familiar Saxon, " dust " ?

(*Pause, with expression on faces of sorrowful doubt ;* LILY *gives voice to the general sentiment in a timid* " *Please don't.*")

No, children, I won't call you that ; and
mind, as you grow up, that you do not get
into an idle and wicked habit of calling
yourselves that.   You are something better
than dust, and have other duties to do than
ever dust can do ; and the bonds of affec-
tion you will enter into are better than
merely "getting into order."   But see to it, on
the other hand, that you always behave at
least as well as "dust :" remember, it is only
on compulsion, and while it has no free permission to do as it likes, that *it* ever gets
out of order ; but sometimes, with some of
us, the compulsion has to be the other way
—hasn't it ? (*Remonstratory whispers, ex-
pressive of opinion that the* LECTURER *is becoming too personal.*)   I'm not looking at
anybody in particular—indeed I am not.
Nay, if you blush so, Kathleen, how can
one help looking?   We'll go back to the
atoms.

"How do they know their places ?" you
asked, or should have asked.   Yes, and they
have to do much more than know them :
they have to find their way to them, and
that quietly and at once, without running
against each other.

We may, indeed, state it briefly thus :—
Suppose you have to build a castle, with
towers and roofs and buttresses, out of
bricks of a given shape, and that these
bricks are all lying in a huge heap at the
bottom, in utter confusion, upset out of

carts at random. You would have to draw
a great many plans, and count all your
bricks, and be sure you had enough for this
and that tower, before you began, and then
you would have to lay your foundation, and add layer by layer, in order,
slowly.

But how would you be astonished in
these melancholy days, when children don't
read children's books, nor believe any more
in fairies, if suddenly a real benevolent
fairy, in a bright brick-red gown, were to
rise in the midst of the red bricks, and to
tap the heap of them with her wand, and
say, "Bricks, bricks, to your places!" and
then you saw in an instant the whole heap
rise in the air, like a swarm of red bees,
and—you have been used to see bees make
a honeycomb, and to think that strange
enough, but now you would see the honeycomb make itself!—You want to ask
something, Florrie, by the look of your
eyes.

FLORRIE. Are they turned into real bees,
with stings?

L. No, Florrie; you are only to fancy
flying bricks, as you saw the slates flying
from the roof the other day in the storm;
only those slates didn't seem to know where
they were going, and, besides, were going,
where they had no business : but my spell-
bound bricks, though they have no wings,
and, what is worse, no heads and no eyes,

yet find their way in fhe air just where they should settle, into towers and roofs, each flying to his place and fastening there at the right moment, so that every other one shall fit to him in his turn.

LILY. But who are the fairies, then, who build the crystals?

L. There is one great fairy, Lily, who builds much more than crystals; but she builds these also. I dreamed that I saw her building a pyramid, the other day, as she used to do, for the Pharaohs.

ISABEL. But that was only a dream?

L. Some dreams are truer than some wakings, Isabel; but I won't tell it you unless you like.

ISABEL. Oh, please, please.

L. You are all such wise children, there's no talking to you; you won't believe anything.

LILY. No, we are not wise, and we will believe anything, when you say we ought.

L. Well, it came about this way. Sibyl, do you recollect that evening when we had been looking at your old cave by Cumæ, and wondering why you didn't live there still: and then we wondered how old you were; and Egypt said you wouldn't tell, and nobody else could tell but she; and you laughed—I thought very gayly for a Sibyl—and said you would harness a flock of cranes for us, and we might fly over to Egypt if we liked, and see.

SIBYL. Yes, and you went, and couldn't find out after all !

L. Why, you know, Egypt had been just doubling that third pyramid of hers ; * and making a new entrance into it ; and a fine entrance it was ! First, we had to go through an ante-room, which had both its doors blocked up with stones ; and then we had three granite portcullises to pull up, one after another ; and the moment we had got under them, Egypt signed to somebody above ; and down they came again behind us, with a roar like thunder, only louder ; then we got into a passage fit for nobody but rats, and Egypt wouldn't go any further herself, but said we might go on if we liked ; and so we came to a hole in the pavement, and then to a granite trap-door —and then we thought we had gone quite far enough, and came back, and Egypt laughed at us.

EGYPT. You would not have had me take my crown off, and stoop all the way down a passage fit only for rats ?

L. It was not the crown, Egypt—you know that very well. It was the flounces that would not let you go any farther. I suppose, however, you wear them as typical of the inundation of the Nile, so it is all right.

ISABEL. Why didn't you take me with

* Note L.

you? Where rats can go, mice can. I wouldn't have come back.

L. No, mousie; you would have gone on by yourself, and you might have waked one of Pasht's cats,* and it would have eaten you. I was very glad you were not there. But after all this I suppose the imagination of the heavy granite blocks and the underground ways had troubled me, and dreams are often shaped in a strange opposition to the impressions that have caused them; and from all that we had been reading in Bunsen about stones that couldn't be lifted with levers, I began to dream about stones that lifted themselves with wings.

Sibyl. Now you must just tell us all about it.

L. I dreamed that I was standing beside the lake, out of whose clay the bricks were made for the great pyramid of Asychis.† They had just been all finished, and were lying by the lake margin, in long ridges, like waves. It was near evening; and as I looked towards the sunset, I saw a thing like a dark pillar standing where the rock of the desert stoops to the Nile valley. I did not know there was a pillar there, and wondered at it; and it grew larger, and glided nearer, becoming like the form of a man, but vast, and it did not move its feet, but glided, like a pillar of sand. And as it

* Note iii.   † Note ii.

3

drew nearer, I looked by chance past it, towards the sun ; and saw a silver cloud, which was of all the clouds closest to the sun (and in one place crossed it), draw itself back from the sun, suddenly. And it turned, and shot towards the dark pillar ; leaping in an arch, like an arrow out of a bow. And I thought it was lightning ; but when it came near the shadowy pillar, it sank slowly down beside it, and changed into the shape of a woman, very beautiful, and with a strength of deep calm in her blue eyes. She was robed to the feet with a white robe ; and above that, to her knees, by the cloud which I had seen across the sun ; but all the golden ripples of it had become plumes, so that it had changed into two bright wings like those of a vulture, which wrapped round her to her knees. She had a weaver's shuttle hanging over her shoulder, by the thread of it, and in her left hand, arrows, tipped with fire.

ISABEL (*clapping her hands*). Oh ! it was Neith, it was Neith ! I know now.

L. Yes ; it was Neith herself ; and as the two great spirits came nearer to me, I saw they were the Brother and Sister—the pillared shadow was the greater Pthah.* And I heard them speak, and the sound of their words was like a distant singing. I could not understand the words one by one ; yet their sense came to me ; and so I knew that

* Note iii.

Neith had come down to see her brother's work, and the work that he had put into the mind of the king to make his servants do. And she was displeased at it; because she saw only pieces of dark clay; and no porphyry, nor marble, nor any fair stone that men might engrave the figures of the gods upon. And she blamed her brother, and said, "Oh, Lord of truth! is this then thy will, that men should mold only four-square pieces of clay: and the forms of the gods no more?" Then the Lord of truth sighed, and said, "Oh! sister, in truth they do not love us; why should they set up our images? Let them do what they may, and not lie—let them make their clay four-square; and labor; and perish."

Then Neith's dark blue eyes grew darker, and she said, "Oh, Lord of truth! why should they love us? their love is vain; or fear us? for their fear is base. Yet let them testify of us, that they knew we lived forever."

But the Lord of truth answered, "They know, and yet they know not. Let them keep silence; for their silence only is truth."

But Neith answered, "Brother, wilt thou also make league with Death, because Death is true? Oh! thou potter, who hast cast these human things from thy wheel, many to dishonor, and few to honor; wilt thou not let them so much as see my face; but slay them in slavery?"

But Pthah only answered, "Let them build, sister, let them build."

And Neith answered, "What shall they build, if I build not with them?"

And Pthah drew with his measuring rod upon the sand. And I saw suddenly, drawn on the sand, the outlines of great cities, and of vaults, and domes, and aqueducts, and bastions, and towers, greater than obelisks, covered with black clouds. And the wind blew ripples of sand amidst the lines that Pthah drew, and the moving sand was like the marching of men. But I saw that wherever Neith looked at the lines, they faded, and were effaced.

"Oh, Brother!" she said at last, "what is this vanity? If I, who am Lady of wisdom, do not mock the children of men, why shouldst thou mock them who art Lord of truth?" But Pthah answered, "They thought to bind me; and they shall be bound. They shall labor in the fire for vanity."

And Neith said, looking at the sand, "Brother, there is no true labor here—there is only weary life and wasteful death."

And Pthah answered, "Is it not truer labor, sister, than thy sculpture of dreams?"

Then Neith smiled; and stopped suddenly.

She looked to the sun; its edge touched the horizon-edge of the desert. Then she looked to the long heaps of pieces of clay that lay, each with its blue shadow, by the lake shore.

" Brother," she said, "how long will this pyramid of thine be in building ? "

"Thoth will have sealed the scroll of the years ten times, before the summit is laid."

"Brother, thou knowest not how to teach thy children to labor," answered Neith, "Look ! I must follow Phre beyond Atlas; shall I build your pyramid for you before he goes down ?" And Pthah answered, "Yea, sister, if thou canst put thy winged shoulders to such work." And Neith drew herself to her height; and I heard a clashing pass through the plumes of her wings, and the asp stood up on her helmet, and fire gathered in her eye. And she took one of the flaming arrows out of the sheaf in her left hand, and stretched it out over the heaps of clay. And they rose up like flights of locusts, and spread themselves in the air, so that it grew dark in a moment. Then Neith designed them places with her arrow point ; and they drew into ranks, like dark clouds laid level at morning. Then Neith pointed with her arrow to the north, and to the south, and to the east, and to the west ; and the flying motes of earth drew asunder into four great ranked crowds ; and stood, one in the north, and one in the south, and one in the east, and one in the west—one against another. Then Neith spread her wings wide for an instant, and closed them with a sound like the sound of a rushing sea; and waved her hand towards the foundation of the pyramid, where it was laid on the brow of the desert. And the four flocks drew together and sank down, like sea-birds settling to a level rock, and when they met, there was a sudden flame, as broad as the pyramid, and as high as the clouds; and it dazzled me; and I closed my eyes for an instant; and when I looked again the pyramid stood on its rock, perfect; and purple with the light from the edge of the sinking sun.

THE YOUNGER CHILDREN (*variously pleased*). I'm so glad! How nice! But what did Pthah say?

L. Neith did not wait to hear what he would say. When I turned back to look at her, she was gone; and I only saw the level white cloud form itself again, close to the arch of the sun as it sank. And as the last edge of the sun disappeared, the form of Pthah faded into a mighty shadow, and so passed away.

EGYPT. And was Neith's pyramid left?

L. Yes; but you could not think, Egypt, what a strange feeling of utter loneliness came over me when the presence of the two gods passed away. It seemed as if I had never known what it was to be alone before; and the unbroken line of the desert was terrible.

EGYPT. I used to feel that, when I was

queen : sometimes I had to carve gods for company, all over my palace. I would fain have seen real ones, if I could.

L. But listen a moment yet, for that was not quite all my dream. The twilight drew swiftly to the dark, and I could hardly see the great pyramid ; when there came a heavy murmuring sound in the air ; and a horned beetle, with terrible claws, fell on the sand at my feet, with a blow like the beat of a hammer. Then it stood up on its hind claws, and waved its pincers at me : and its fore claws became strong arms, and hands ; one grasping real iron pincers, and the other a huge hammer ; and it had a helmet on its head, without any eyelet holes, that I could see. And its two hind claws became strong crooked legs, with feet bent inwards. And so there stood by me a dwarf, in glossy black armor, ribbed and embossed like a beetle's back, leaning on his hammer. And I could not speak for wonder ; but he spoke with a murmur like the dying away of a beat upon a bell. He said, "I will make Neith's great pyramid small. I am the lower Pthah ; and have power over fire. I can wither the strong things, and strengthen the weak ; and everything that is great I can make small, and everything that is little I can make great." Then he turned to the angle of the pyramid and limped towards it. And the pyramid grew deep purple ; and then red like blood, and then pale rose-color like fire. And I saw that it glowed with fire from within. And the lower Pthah touched it with the hand that held the pincers; and it sank down like the sand in an hour-glass,—then drew itself together, and sank, still, and became nothing, it seemed to me ; but the armed dwarf stooped down, and took it into his hand, and brought it to me saying, "Everything that is great I can make like this pyramid ; and give into men's hands to destroy." And I saw that he had a little pyramid in his hand, with as many courses in it as the large one ; and built like that,— only so small. And because it glowed still, I was afraid to touch it ; but Pthah said, "Touch it—for I have bound the fire within it, so that it cannot burn." So I touched it, and took it into my own hand ; and it was cold ; only red, like a ruby. And Pthah laughed, and became like a beetle again, and buried himself in the sand, fiercely ; throwing it back over his shoulders. And it seemed to me as if he would draw me down with him into the sand ; and I started back, and woke holding the little pyramid so fast in my hand that it hurt me.

EGYPT. Holding WHAT in your hand?

L. The little pyramid.

EGYPT. Neith's pyramid?

L. Neith's, I believe ; though not built for Asychis. I know only that it is a little rosy transparent pyramid, built of more courses.

of bricks than I can count, it being made so
small.   You don't believe me, of course,
Egyptian infidel ; but there it is.   (*Giving
crystal of rose Fluor.*)

> (*Confused examination by crowded audi-
> ence, over each other's shoulders and
> under each other's arms.   Disappoint-
> mentbegins to manifest itself.*)

SIBYL (*not quite knowing why she and
others are disappointed*).   But you showed us
this the other day.

L. Yes ; but you would not look at it the
other day.

SIBYL. But was all that fine dream only
about this ?

L. What finer thing could a dream be
about than this ?   It is small, if you will ;
but when you begin to think of things
rightly, the ideas of smallness and largeness
pass away.   The making of this pyramid
was in reality just as wonderful as the dream
I have been telling you, and just as incom-
prehensible.   It was not, I suppose, as
swift, but quite as grand things are done
as swiftly.   When Neith makes crystals of
snow it needs a great deal more marshaling
of the atoms, by her flaming arrows, than it
does to make crystals like this one ; and that
is done in a moment.

EGYPT. But how you *do* puzzle us !   Why
do you say Neith does it ?   You don't mean
that she is a real spirit, do you ?

L. What *I* mean, is of little consequence. What the Egyptians meant, who called her "Neith,"—or Homer, who called her "Athena,"—or Solomon, who called her by a word which the Greeks render as "Sophia," you must judge for yourselves. But her testimony is always the same, and all nations have received it: "I was by Him as one brought up with Him, and I was daily His delight; rejoicing in the habitual parts of the earth, and my delights were with the sons of men."

MARY. But is not that only a personification?

L. If it be, what will you gain by unpersonifying it, or what right have you to do so? Cannot you accept the image given you, in its life; and listen, like children, to the words which chiefly belong to you as children: "I love them that love me, and those that seek me early shall find me"?

(They are all quiet for a minute or two; questions begin to appear in their eyes.)

I cannot talk to you any more to-day. Take that rose-crystal away with you, and think.

LECTURE 3.

THE CRYSTAL LIFE.

LECTURE

THE CRYSTAL LIFE.

A very dull Lecture, willfully brought upon themselves by the elder children. Some of the young ones have, however, managed to get in by mistake. SCENE, the schoolroom.

L. So I am to stand up here merely to be asked questions, to-day, Miss Mary, am I?

MARY. Yes; and you must answer them plainly; without telling us any more stories. You are quite spoiling the children : the poor little things' heads are turning round like kaleidoscopes ; and they don't know in the least what you mean. Nor do we old ones either, for that matter: to-day you must really tell us nothing but facts.

L. I am sworn ; but you won't like it a bit.

MARY. Now, first of all, what do you mean by "bricks" ?—Are the smallest particles of minerals all of some accurate shape, like bricks?

L. I do not know, Miss Mary; I do not even know if anybody knows. The smallest atoms which are visibly and practically put together to make large crystals, may

45

better be described as "limited in fixed directions" than as "of fixed forms." But I can
tell you nothing clear about ultimate atoms ;
you will find the idea of little bricks, or, perhaps, of little spheres, available for all the
uses you will have to put it to.

MARY. Well, it's very provoking ; one
seems always to be stopped just when one
is coming to the very thing one wants to
know.

L. No, Mary, for we should not wish to
know anything but what is easily and assuredly knowable. There's no end to it.
If I could show you, or myself, a group of
ultimate atoms, quite clearly, in this magnifying glass, we should both be presently
vexed because we could not break them in
two pieces, and see their insides.

MARY. Well, then, next, what do you mean
by the flying of the bricks ? What is it the
atoms do, that is like flying ?

L. When they are dissolved, or uncrystal-
lized, they are really separated from each
other, like a swarm of gnats in the air, or
like a shoal of fish in the sea ;—generally at
about equal distances. In currents of solu-
tions, or at different depths of them, one
part may be more full of the dissolved
atoms than another ; but on the whole, you
may think of them as equidistant, like the
spots in the print of your gown. If they are
separated by force of heat only, the substance is said to be melted ; if they are sep-

arated by any other substance, as particles
of sugar by water, they are said to be "dissolved." Note this distinction carefully, all
of you.

DORA. I will be very particular. When
next you tell me there isn't sugar enough in
your tea, I will say, "It is not yet dissolved,
sir."

L. I tell you what shall be dissolved, Miss
Dora; and that's the present parliament, if
the members get too saucy.

(DORA *folds her hands and casts down
her eyes.*)

L. (*proceeds in state*). Now, Miss Mary,
you know already, I believe, that nearly
everything will melt, under a sufficient heat,
like wax. Limestone melts (under pressure);
sand melts; granite melts; the lava of a
volcano is a mixed mass of many kinds of
rocks, melted: and any melted substance
nearly always, if not always, crystallizes as
it cools; the more slowly the more perfectly. Water melts at what we call the freez-
ing, but might just as wisely, though not as
conveniently, call the melting, point; and
radiates as it cools into the most beautiful
of all known crystals. Glass melts at a
greater heat, and will crystallize, if you will
let it cool slowly enough, in stars, much
like snow. Gold needs more heat to melt
it, but crystallizes also exquisitely, as I will
presently show you. Arsenic and sulphur
crystallizes from their vapors. Now in any

of these cases, either of melted, dissolved, or
vaporous bodies, the particles are usually
separated from each other, either by heat
or by an intermediate substance ; and in
crystallizing they are both brought nearer
to each other, and packed, so as to fit as
closely as possible : the essential part of
the business being not the bringing together,
but the packing. Who packed your trunk
for you, last holidays, Isabel ?

ISABEL. Lily does, always.

L. And how much can you allow for
Lily's good packing, in guessing what will
go into the trunk?

ISABEL. Oh ! I bring twice as much as the
trunk holds. Lily always gets everything in.

LILY. Ah ! but, Isey, if you only knew
what a time it takes ! and since you've had
those great hard buttons on your frocks, I
can't do anything with them.   Buttons
won't go anywhere, you know.

L. Yes, Lily, it would be well if she only
knew what a time it takes ; and I wish any
of us knew what a time crystallization takes,
for that is consummately fine packing.   The
particles of the rock are thrown down, just
as Isabel brings her things—in a heap ; and
innumerable Lilies, not of the valley, but of
the rock, come to pack them.   But it takes
such a time !

However, the best—out and out the best
—way of understanding the thing, is to crystallize yourselves.

THE AUDIENCE. Ourselves!

L. Yes ; not merely as you did the other day, carelessly on the schoolroom forms ; but carefully and finely, out in the playground. You can play at crystallization there as much as you please.

KATHLEEN *and* JESSIE. Oh! how?—how?

L. First you must put yourselves together as close as you can, in the middle of the grass, and form for first practice, any figure you like.

JESSIE. Any dancing figure, do you mean?

L. No ; I mean a square, or a cross, or a diamond. Any figure you like, standing close together. You had better outline it first on the turf, with sticks, or pebbles, so as to see that it is rightly drawn ; then get into it and enlarge or diminish it at one side, till you are all quite in it, and no empty space left.

DORA. Crinoline and all ?

L. The crinoline may stand eventually for rough crystalline surface, unless you pin it in ; and then you may make a polished crystal of yourselves.

LILY. Oh, we'll pin it in—we'll pin it in !

L. Then, when you are all in the figure, let every one note her place, and who is next her on each side ; and let the outsiders count how many places they stand from the corners.

KATHLEEN. Yes, yes,—and then?

L. Then you must scatter all over the

4

playground—right over it from side to side, and end to end ; and put yourselves all at equal distances from each other, everywhere. You needn't mind doing it very accurately, but so as to be nearly equidistant ; not less than about three yards apart from each other on every side.

JESSIE. We can easily cut pieces of string of equal length, to hold.   And then ?

L. Then, at a given signal, let everybody walk, at the same rate, towards the outlined figure in the middle.   You had better sing as you walk ; that will keep you in good time.   And as you close in towards it, let each take her place, and the next comers fit themselves in beside the first ones, till you are all in the figure again.

KATHLEEN. Oh ! how we shall run against each other.   What fun it will be !

L. No, no, Miss Katie ; I can't allow any running against each other.   The atoms never do that, whatever human creatures do.   You must all know your places, and find your way to them without jostling.

LILY. But how ever shall we do that ?

ISABEL. Mustn't the ones in the middle be the nearest, and the outside ones farther off —when we go away to scatter, I mean ?

L. Yes ; you must be very careful to keep your order ; you will soon find out how to do it ; it is only like soldiers forming square, except that each must stand still in her place as she reaches it, and the others come round

her ; and you will have much more com-
plicated figures, afterwards to form, than
squares.

ISABEL. I'll put a stone at my place : then
I shall know it.

L. You might each nail a bit of paper to
the turf, at your place, with your name upon it : but it would be of no use, for if you
don't know your places, you will make a
fine piece of business of it, while you are
looking for your names.   And, Isabel, if with
a little head and eyes, and a brain (all of
them very good and serviceable of their kind,
as such things go), you think you cannot
know your place, without a stone at it, after
examining it well,—how do you think each
atom knows its place, when it never was
there before, and there's no stone at it ?

ISABEL. But does every atom know its
place ?

L. How else could it get there ?

MARY. Are they not attracted into their
places ?

L. Cover a piece of paper with spots, at
equal intervals ; and then imagine any kind
of attraction you choose, or any law of attraction, to exist between the spots, and try
how, on that permitted supposition, you can
attract them into the figure of a Maltese
cross, in the middle of the paper.

MARY (*having tried it*).   Yes ; I see that I
cannot :—one would need all kinds of at-
tractions, in different ways, at different

places.   But you do not mean that the atoms
are alive?

L. What is it to be alive?

DORA. There now; you're going to be
provoking, I know.

L. I do not see why it should be provoking to be asked what it is to be alive.   Do
you think you don't know whether you are
alive or not?

(ISABEL *skips to the end of the room and
back.*)

L. Yes, Isabel, that's all very fine; and
you and I may call that being alive: but a
modern philosopher calls it being in a
"mood of motion."   It requires a certain
quantity of heat to take you to the side-
board; and exactly the same quantity to
bring you back again.   That's all.

ISABEL. No, it isn't.   And besides, I'm not
hot.

L. I am, sometimes, at the way they talk.
However, you know, Isabel, you might have
been a particle of a mineral, and yet have
been carried round the room, or anywhere
else, by chemical forces, in the liveliest way.

ISABEL. Yes; but I wasn't carried: I carried myself.

L. The fact is, mousie, the difficulty is
not so much to say what makes a thing
alive, as what makes it a Self.   As soon as
you are shut off from the rest of the universe
into a Self, you begin to be alive.

VIOLET (*indginant*). Oh, surely—surely
that cannot be so.   Is not all the life of the
soul in communion, not separation?

L. There can be no communion where
there is no distinction.   But we shall be in
an abyss of metaphysics presently, if we
don't look out ; and besides, we must not be
too grand, to-day, for the younger children.
We'll be grand, some day, by ourselves, if
we must.   (*The younger children are not
pleased, and prepare to remonstrate ; but knowing by experience, that all conversations in
which the word "communion" occurs, are
unintelligible, think better of it.*)   Meantime,
for broad answer about the atoms.   I do not
think we should use the word "life," of any
energy which does not belong to a given
form.   A seed, or an egg, or a young animal,
are properly called "alive" with respect to
the force belonging to those forms, which
consistently develops that form, and no
other.   But the force which crystallizes a
mineral appears to be chiefly external, and
it does not produce an entirely determinate
and individual form, limited in size, but only
an aggregation, in which some limiting laws
must be observed.

MARY. But I do not see much difference,
that way, between a crystal and a tree.

L. Add, then, that the mode of the energy
in a living thing implies a continual change
in its elements ; and a period for its end.
So you may define life by its attached nega-

tive, death ; and still more by its attached
positive, birth.   But I won't be plagued any
more about this, just now ; if you choose
to think the crystals alive, do, and welcome.
Rocks have always been called "living" in
their native place.

MARY. There's one question more; then
I've done.

L. Only one?

MARY. Only one.

L. But if it is answered won't it turn into
two ?

MARY. No ; I think it will remain single,
and be comfortable.

L. Let me hear it.

MARY. You know, we are to crystallize
ourselves out of the whole playground.
Now, what playground have the minerals ?
Where are they scattered before they are
crystallized ; and where are the crystals
generally made ?

L. That sounds to me more like three
questions than one, Mary. If it is only
one, it is a wide one.

MARY. I did not say anything about the
width of it

L. Well, I must keep it within the best
compass I can.   When rocks either dry from
a moist state, or cool from a heated state,
they necessarily alter in bulk ; and cracks, or
open spaces, form in them in all directions.
These cracks must be filled up with solid
matter, or the rock would eventually be-

come a ruinous heap. So, sometimes by water, sometimes by vapor, sometimes nobody knows how, crystallizable matter is brought from somewhere, and fastens itself in these open spaces, so as to bind the rock together again with crystal cement. A vast quantity of hollows are formed in lavas by bubbles of gas, just as the holes are left in bread well-baked. In process of time these cavities are generally filled with various crystals.

MARY. But where does the crystallizing substance come from ?

L. Sometimes out of the rock itself; sometimes from below or above, through the veins. The entire substance of the contracting rock may be filled with liquid, pressed into it so as to fill every pore ;—or with mineral vapor ;—or it may be so charged at one place, and empty at another. There's no end to the "may be's." But all that you need fancy, for our present purpose, is that hollows in the rocks, like the caves in Derbyshire, are traversed by liquids or vapor containing certain elements in a more or less free or separate state, which crystallize on the cave walls.

SIBYL. There now ;—Mary has had all her questions answered; it's my turn to have mine.

L. Ah, there's a conspiracy among you, I see. I might have guessed as much.

DORA. I'm sure you ask us questions

enough! How can you have the heart, when you dislike so to be asked them yourself?

L. My dear child, if people do not answer questions, it does not matter how many they are asked, because they've no trouble with them. Now, when I ask you questions, I never expect to be answered; but when you ask me, you always do; and it's not fair.

DORA. Very well, we shall understand, next time.

SIBYL. No, but seriously, we all want to ask one thing more, quite dreadfully.

L. And I don't want to be asked it, quite dreadfully; but you'll have your own way, of course.

SIBYL. We none of us understand about the lower Pthah. It was not merely yesterday; but in all we have read about him in Wilkinson, or in any book, we cannot understand what the Egyptians put their god into that ugly little deformed shape for.

L. Well, I'm glad it's that sort of question; because I can answer anything I like to that.

EGYPT. Anything you like will do quite well for us; we shall be pleased with the answer, if you are.

L. I am not so sure of that, most gracious queen; for I must begin by the statement that queens seem to have disliked all sorts of work, in those days, as much as some queens dislike sewing to-day.

EGYPT. Now, it's too bad! and just when I was trying to say the civilest thing I could!

L. But, Egypt, why did you tell me you disliked sewing so?

EGYPT. Did not I show you how the thread cuts my fingers? and I always get cramp, somehow, in my neck, if I sew long.

L. Well, I suppose the Egyptian queens thought everybody got cramp in their neck, if they sewed long; and that thread always cut people's fingers. At all events every kind of manual labor was despised both by them, and the Greeks; and, while they owned the real good and fruit of it, they yet held it a degradation to all who practiced it. Also, knowing the laws of life thoroughly, they perceived that the special practice necessary to bring any manual art to perfection strengthened the body distortedly; one energy or member gaining at the expense of the rest. They especially dreaded and despised any kind of work that had to be done near fire: yet feeling what they owed to it in metal-work, as the basis of all other work, they expressed this mixed reverence and scorn in the varied types of the lame Hephæstus, and the lower Pthah.

SIBYL. But what did you mean by making him say "Everything great I can make small, and everything small great"?

L. I had my own separate meaning in that. We have seen in modern times the

power of the lower Pthah developed in a
separate way, which no Greek nor Egyptian
could have conceived. It is the character
of pure and eyeless manual labor to conceive everything as subjected to it ; and in
reality to disgrace and diminish all that is
so subjected, aggrandizing itself, and the
thought of itself, at the expense of all noble
things. I heard an orator, and a good one
too, at the Working Men's College, the other
day, make a great point in a description of
our railroads ; saying, with grandly con-
ducted emphasis, "They have made man
greater, and the world less." His working
audience were mightily pleased ; they
thought it so very fine a thing to be made
bigger themselves ; and all the rest of the
world less. I should have enjoyed asking
them (but it would have been a pity—they
were so pleased), how much less they would
like to have the world made ;—and whether,
at present, those of them really felt the big-
gest men, who lived in the least houses.

SIBYL. But then, why did you make Pthah
say that he could make weak things strong,
and small things great?

L. My dear, he is a boaster and self-as-
sertor, by nature ; but it is so far true. For
instance, we used to have a fair in our
neighborhood—a very fine fair we thought it.
You never saw such an one ; but if you look
at the engraving of Turner's "St Catherine's
Hill," you will see what it was like. There

were curious booths, carried on poles ; and
peep-shows ; and music, with plenty of drums
and cymbals ; and much barley-sugar and
ginger bread, and the like : and in the alleys
of this fair the London populace would enjoy
themselves, after their fashion, very thoroughly.   Well, the little Pthah set to work
upon it one day ; he make the wooden poles
into iron ones, and put them across, like his
own crooked legs, so that you always fall
over them if you don't look where you are
going ; and he turned all the canvas into
panes of glass, and put it up on his iron
cross-poles ; and made all the little booths
into one great booth ;—and people said it
was very fine, and a new style of architecture ; and Mr. Dickens said nothing was
ever like it in Fairy-land, which was very
true.   And then the little Pthah set to work
to put fine fairings in it ; and he painted the
Nineveh bulls afresh, with the blackest eyes
he could paint (because he had none himself), and he got the angels down from
Lincoln choir, and gilded their wings like
his gingerbread of old times ; and he sent
for everything else he could think of, and
put it in his booth.   There are the casts of
Niobe and her children ; and the Chim-
panzee ; and the wooden Caffres and New-
Zealanders ; and the Shakespeare House ;
and Le Grand Blondin, and Le Petit Blondin ;
and Handel ; and Mozart ; and no end of
shops, and buns, and beer ; and all the little-

Pthah-worshippers say, never was anything
so sublime !

Sibyl. Now, do you mean to say you
never go to these Crystal Palace concerts ;
they're as good as good can be.

L. I don't go to the thundering things
with a million of bad voices in them.   When
I want a song, I get Julia Mannering and
Lucy Bertram and Counselor Pleydell to
sing "We be three poor Mariners" to me;
then I've no headache next morning.   But
I do go to the smaller concerts, when I can ;
for they are very good, as you say, Sibyl :
and I always get a reserved seat somewhere
near the orchestra, where I am sure I can
see the kettle-drummer drum.

Sibyl. Now *do* be serious, for one minute.

L. I am serious—never was more so.
You know one can't see the modulation of
violinists' fingers, but one can see the vibra-
tion of the drummer's hand : and it's lovely.

Sibyl. But fancy going to a concert, not
to hear, but to see !

L. Yes, it is very absurd.   The quite
right thing, I believe, is to go there to talk.
I confess, however, that in most music,
when very well done, the doing of it is to
me the chiefly interesting part of the business.   I'm always thinking how good it
would be for the fat, supercilious people,
who care so little for their half-crown's worth,
to be set to try and do a half-crown's worth
of anything like it.

MARY. But surely that Crystal Palace is a
great good and help to the people of London?

L. The fresh air of the Norwood hills is,
or was, my dear; but they are spoiling that
with smoke as fast as they can. And the
palace (as they call it) is a better place for
them, by much, than the old fair; and it is
always there, instead of for three days only;
and it shuts up at proper hours of night.
And good use may be made of the things in
it, if you know how: but as for its teaching
the people, it will teach them nothing but
the lowest of the lower Pthah's work—nothing but hammer and tongs. I saw a wonderful piece of his doing in the place, only
the other day. Some unhappy metal-worker
—I am not sure if it was not a metal-work-
ing firm—had taken three years to make a
Golden eagle.

SIBYL. Of real gold?

L. No; of bronze, or copper, or some of
their foul patent metals—it is no matter
what. I meant a model of our chief British
eagle. Every feather was made separately;
and every filament of every feather separately, and so joined on; and all the quills
modeled of the right length and right sec-
tion, and at last the whole cluster of them
fastened together. You know, children, I
don't think much of my own drawing; but
take my proud word for once, that when I
go to the Zoological Gardens, and happen

to have a bit of chalk in my pocket, and the Gray Harpy will sit, without screwing his head round, for thirty seconds,—I can do a better thing of him in that time than the three years' work of this industrious firm. For, during the thirty seconds, the eagle is my object,—not myself; and during the three years, the firm's object, in every fiber of bronze it made, was itself, and not the eagle.   That is the true meaning of the little Pthah's having no eyes—he can see only himself.   The Egyptian beetle was not quite the full type of him ; our northern ground beetle is a truer one.   It is beautiful to see it at work, gathering its treasures (such as they are) into little round balls ; and pushing them home with the strong wrong end of it,—head downmost all the way,—like a modern political economist with his ball of capital, declaring that a nation can stand on its vices better than on its virtues.   But away with you, children, now, for I'm getting cross.

DORA. I'm going downstairs ; I shall take care, at any rate, that there are no little Pthahs in the kitchen cupboards.

THE CRYSTAL ORDERS.

LECTURE IV.

THE CRYSTAL ORDERS.

A working Lecture in the large Schoolroom ; with experimental Interludes. The great bell has rung unexpectedly.

KATHLEEN (*entering disconsolate, though first at the summons*). Oh dear, oh dear, what a day ! Was ever anything so provoking! just when we wanted to crystallize ourselves;—and I'm sure it's going to rain all day long.

L. So am I, Kate. The sky has quite an Irish way with it. But I don't see why Irish girls should also look so dismal. Fancy that you don't want to crystallize yourselves : you didn't, the day before yesterday, and you were not unhappy when it rained then.

FLORRIE. Ah ! but we do want to-day ; and the rain's so tiresome.

L. That is to say, children, that because you are all the richer by the expectation of playing at a new game, you choose to make yourselves unhappier than when you had nothing to look forward to, but the old ones.

ISABEL. But then, to have to wait—wait —wait ; and before we've tried it ;—and perhaps it will rain to-morrow, too !

5

L. It may also rain the day after to-morrow. We can make ourselves uncomfortable to any extent with perhapses, Isabel. You may stick perhapses into your little minds, like pins, till you are as uncomfortable as the Lilliputians made Gulliver with their arrows, when he would not lie quiet.

ISABEL. But what *are* we to do to-day?

L. To be quiet, for one thing, like Gulliver when he saw there was nothing better to be done. And to practice patience. I can tell you, children, *that* requires nearly as much practicing as music; and we are continually losing our lessons when the master comes. Now, to-day, here's a nice, little adagio lesson for us, if we play it properly.

ISABEL. But I don't like that sort of lesson. I can't play it properly.

L. Can you play a Mozart sonata yet, Isabel? The more need to practice. All one's life is a music, if one touches the notes rightly, and in time. But there must be no hurry.

KATHLEEN. I'm sure there's no music in stopping in on a rainy day.

L. There's no music in a "rest," Katie, that I know of: but there's the making of music in it. And people are always missing that part of the life-melody; and scrambling on without counting—not that it's easy to count; but nothing on which so much depends ever *is* easy. People are always talking of perseverance, and courage, and fortitude ; but patience is the finest and worthiest part of fortitude,—and the rarest, too. I know twenty persevering girls for one patient one : but it is only that twenty-first who can do her work, out and out, or enjoy it. . For patience lies at the root of all pleasures, as well as of all powers. Hope herself ceases to be happiness, when Impatience companions her.

> ISABEL and LILY *sit down on the floor and fold their hands. The others follow their example.*)

Good children ! but that's not quite the way of it, neither. Folded hands are not necessarily resigned ones. The Patience who really smiles at grief usually stands, or walks, or even runs : she seldom sits ; though she may sometimes have to do it for many a day, poor thing, by monuments ; or like Chaucer's, "with face pale, upon a hill of sand." But we are not reduced to that to-day. Suppose we use this calamitous forenoon to choose the shapes we are to crystallize into ? we know nothing about them yet.

> *The pictures of resignation rise from the floor not in the patientest manner. General applause.*)

MARY (*with one or two others*). The very thing we wanted to ask you about !

LILY. We looked at the books about crystals, but they are so dreadful.

L. Well, Lily, we must go through a little dreadfulness, that's a fact : no road to any good knowledge is wholly among the lilies and the grass ; there is rough climbing to be done always. But the crystal-books are a little *too* dreadful, most of them, I admit ; and we shall have to be content with very little of their help. You know, as you cannot stand on each other's heads, you can only make yourselves into the sections of crystals,—the figures they show when they are cut through ; and we will choose some that will be quite easy. You shall make diamonds of yourselves—

ISABEL. Oh, no, no ! we won't be diamonds, please.

L. Yes, you shall, Isabel ; they are very pretty things, if the jewelers and the kings and queens, would only let them alone. You shall make diamonds of yourselves, and rubies of yourselves, and emeralds ; and Irish diamonds ; two of those—with Lily in the middle of one, which will be very orderly, of course ; and Kathleen in the middle of the other, for which we will hope the best ; and you shall make Derbyshire spar of yourselves, and Iceland spar, and gold, and silver, and— Quicksilver there's enough of in you, without any making.

MARY. Now, you know, the children will be getting quite wild : we must really get pencils and paper, and begin properly.

L. Wait a minute, Miss Mary : I think, as

we've the schoolroom clear to-day, I'll try
to give you some notion of the three great
orders or ranks of crystals, into which all
the others seem more or less to fall. We
shall only want one figure a day, in the
playground; and that can be drawn in a
minute: but the general Ideas had better be
fastened first. I must show you a great
many minerals; so let me have three tables
wheeled into the three windows, that we
may keep our specimens separate ;—we will
keep the three orders of crystals on separate
tables.

(*First Interlude, of pushing and pulling,
and spreading of baize covers.* VIOLET,
*not particularly minding what she is
about, gets herself jammed into a corner, and bid to stand out of the way ;
on which she devotes herself to meditation.*)

VIOLET (*after interval of meditation*). How
strange it is that everything seems to divide
into threes !

L. Everything doesn't divide into threes.
Ivy won't, though shamrock will; and
daisies won't, though lilies will.

VIOLET. But all the nicest things seem to
divide into threes.

L. Violets won't.

VIOLET. No ; I should think not, indeed !
But I mean the great things.

L. I've always heard the globe had four
quarters.

ISABEL. Well; but you know you said it
hadn't any quarters at all. So mayn't it
really be divided into three?

L. If it were divided into no more than
three, on the outside of it, Isabel, it would
be a fine world to live in; and if it were
divided into three in the inside of it, it would
soon be no world to live in at all.

DORA. We shall never get to the crystals,
at this rate. (*Aside to* MARY.) He will get
off into political economy before we know
where we are. (*Aloud.*) But the crystals
are divided into three, then?

L. No; but there are three general notions by which we may best get hold of
them, Then between these notions there
are other notions.

LILY (*alarmed*). A great many? And
shall we have to learn them all?

L. More than a great many—a quite infinite many. So you cannot learn them all.

LILY (*greatly relieved*). Then may we
only learn the three?

L. Certainly; unless, when you have got
those three notions, you want to have some
more notions;—which would not surprise
me. But we'll try for the three, first. Katie,
you broke your coral necklace this morning?

KATHLEEN. Oh! who told you? It was in
jumping. I'm so sorry!

L. I'm very glad. Can you fetch me the
beads of it?

KATHLEEN. I've lost some; here are the rest in my pocket, if I can only get them out.

L. You mean to get them out some day, I suppose; so try now. I want them.

(KATHLEEN *empties her pocket on the floor. The beads disperse. The School disperses also. Second Interlude—hunting piece.*)

L. (*after waiting patiently for a quarter of an hour, to* ISABEL, *who comes up from under the table with her hair all about her ears and the last findable beads in her hand*). Mice are useful little things sometimes. Now, mousie, I want all those beads crystallized. How many ways are there of putting them in order?

ISABEL. Well, first one would string them, I suppose?

L. Yes, that's the first way. You cannot string ultimate atoms; but you can put them in a row, and then they fasten themselves together, somehow, into a long rod or needle. We will call these "*Needle*-crystals." What would be the next way?

ISABEL. I suppose, as we are to get together in the playground, when it stops raining, in different shapes?

L. Yes; put the beads together, then, in the simplest form you can, to begin with. Put them into a square, and pack them close.

ISABEL (*after careful endeavor*). I can't get them closer.

L. That will do. Now you may see, be-
forehand, that if you try to throw yourselves
into square in this confused way, you will
never know your places ; so you had better
consider every square as made of rods, put
side by side. Take four beads of equal size,
first, Isabel; put them into a little square.
That you may consider as made up of two
rods of two beads each. Then you can
make a square a size larger, out of three rods
of three. Then the next square may be a
size larger. How many rods, Lily ?

LILY. Four rods of four beads each, I
suppose.

L. Yes, and then five rods of five, and
so on. But now, look here; make another
square of four beads again. You see they
leave a little opening in the center.

ISABEL. (*pushing two opposite ones closer
together*). Now they don't.

L. No ; but now it isn't a square; and
by pushing the two together you have
pushed the two others farther apart.

ISABEL. And yet, somehow, they all seem
closer than they were !

L. Yes ; for before, each of them only
touched two of the others, but now each of
the two in the middle touches the other
three. Take away one of the outsiders,
Isabel ; now you have three in a triangle—
the smallest triangle you can make out of
the beads. Now put a rod of three beads
on at one side. So, you have a triangle of

six beads ; but just the shape of the first
one. Next a rod of four on the side of
that ; and you have a triangle of ten beads :
then a rod of five on the side of that ; and
you have a triangle of fifteen. Thus you
have a square with five beads on the side,
and a triangle with five beads on the side ;
equal-sided, therefore, like the square. So,
however few or many you may be, you
may soon learn how to crystallize quickly into
these two figures, which are the foundation
of form in the commonest, and therefore
actually the most important as well as in
the rarest, and therefore, by our esteem, the
most important minerals of the world.
Look at this in my hand.

VIOLET. Why, it is leaf gold !

L. Yes ; but beaten by no man's hammer, or rather, not beaten at all, but woven.
Besides, feel the weight of it. There is gold
enough there to gild the walls and ceiling,
if it were beaten thin.

VIOLET. How beautiful ! And it glitters
like a leaf covered with frost.

L. You only think it so beautiful because
you know it is gold. It is not prettier, in
reality, than a bit of brass : for it is Transyl-
vanian gold ; and they say there is a foolish
gnome in the mines there, who is always
wanting to live in the moon, and so alloys
all the gold with a little silver. I don't
know how that may be ; but the silver
always *is* in the gold ; and if he does it, it's

very provoking of him, for no gold is woven so fine anywhere else.

MARY (*who has been looking through her magnifying glass*).   But this is not woven. This is all made of little triangles.

L. Say "patched," then, if you must be so particular.   But if you fancy all those triangles, small as they are (and many of them are infinitely small), made up again of rods, and those of grains, as we built our great triangle of the beads, what word will you take for the manufacture?

MAY. There's no word—it is beyond words.

L. Yes ; and that would matter little, were it not beyond thoughts too.   But, at all events, this yellow leaf of dead gold, shed, not from the ruined woodlands, but the ruined rocks, will help you to remember the second kind of crystals, *Leaf*-crystals, or *Foliated* crystals ; though I show you the form in gold first only to make a strong impression on you, for gold is not generally, or characteristically, crystallized in leaves ; the real type of foliated crystals is this thing, Mica ; which if you once feel well, and break well, you will always know again ; and you will often have occasion to know it, for you will find it everywhere nearly, in hill countries.

KATHLEEN. If we break it well | May we break it?

L. To powder, if you like.

(*Surrenders plate of brown mica to public investigation. Third Interlude. It sustains severely philosophical treatment at all hands.*)

FLORRIE (*to whom the last fragments have descended*). Always leaves, and leaves, and nothing but leaves, or white dust?

L. That dust itself is nothing but finer leaves.

(*Shows them to* FLORRIE *through magnifying glass.*)

ISABEL (*peeping over* FLORRIE's *shoulder*). But then this bit under the glass looks like that bit out of the glass! If we could break this bit under the glass, what would it be like?

L. It would be all leaves still.

ISABEL. And then if we broke those again?

L. All less leaves still.

ISABEL (*impatient*). And if we broke them again, and again, and again, and again, and again?

L. Well, I suppose you would come to a limit, if you could only see it, Notice that the little flakes already differ somewhat from the large ones : because I can bend them up and down, and they stay bent ; while the large flake, though it bent easily a little way, sprang back when you let it go, and broke when you tried to bend it far. And a large mass would not bend at all.

MARY. Would that leaf gold separate into finer leaves, in the same way?

L. No; and therefore, as I told you, it is

not a characteristic specimen of a foliated
crystallization.   The latter triangles are portions of solid crystals, and so they are in
this, which looks like a black mica ; but you
see it is made up of triangles like the gold,
and stands, almost accurately, as an intermediate link, in crystals, between mica and
gold.   Yet this is the commonest, as gold
the rarest, of metals.

MARY.   Is it iron?   I never saw iron so
bright.

L.   It is rust of iron, finely crystallized :
from its resemblance to mica, it is often
called micaceous iron.

KATHLEEN.   May we break this, too ?

L.   No, for I could not easily get such another crystal ; besides, it would not break
like the mica ; it is much harder.   But take
the glass again, and look at the fineness of
the jagged edges of the triangles where they
lap over each other.   The gold has the same ;
but you see them better here, terrace above
terrace, countless, and in successive angles,
like superb fortified bastions.

MAY.   But all foliated crystals are not made
of triangles ?

L.   Far from it ; mica is occasionally so,
but usually of hexagons ; and here is a
foliated crystal made of squares, which will
show you that the leaves of the rock-land
have their summer green, as well as their
autumnal gold.

FLORRIE.   Oh ! oh ! oh ! (*jumps for joy*).

L. Did you never see a bit of green leaf before, Florrie?

FLORRIE. Yes, but never so bright as that, and not in a stone.

L. If you will look at the leaves of the trees in sunshine after a shower, you will find they are much brighter than that ; and surely they are none the worse for being on stalks instead of in stones?

FLORRIE. Yes, but then there are so many of them, one never looks, I suppose.

L. Now you have it, Florrie.

VIOLET (*sighing*). There are so many beautiful things we never see !

L. You need not sigh for that, Violet ; but I will tell you what we should all sigh for—that there are so many ugly things we never see.

VIOLET. But we don't want to see ugly things !

L. You had better say, "We don't want to suffer them." You ought to be glad in thinking how much more beauty God has made, than human eyes can ever see ; but not glad in thinking how much more evil man has made, than his own soul can ever conceive, much more than his hands can ever heal.

VIOLET. I don't understand ;—how is that like the leaves?

L. The same law holds in our neglect of multiplied pain, as in our neglect of multiplied beauty. Florrie jumps for joy at sight of half an inch of a green leaf in a brown stone, and takes more notice of it than of all the green in the wood, and you, or I, or any of us, would be unhappy if any single human creature beside us were in sharp pain ; but we can read, at breakfast, day after day, of men being killed, and of women and children dying of hunger faster than the leaves strew the brooks in Vallombrosa ; —and then go out to play croquet, as if nothing had happened.

MAY. But we do not see the people being killed or dying.

L. You did not see your brother, when you got the telegram the other day, saying he was ill, May ; but you cried for him ; and played no croquet. But we cannot talk of these things now ; and what is more, you must let me talk straight on, for a little while ; and ask no questions till I've done ; for we branch ("exfoliate," I should say, mineralogically) always into something else, —though that's my fault more than yours, but I must go straight on now. You have got a distinct notion, I hope, of leaf-crystals ; and you see the sort of look they have : you can easily remember that "folium" is Latin for a leaf, and that the separate flakes of mica, or any other such stones, are called "folia ;" but, because mica is the most characteristic of these stones, other things that are like it in structure are called "micas ;" thus we have Uran-mica, which is the green leaf I showed you ; and Copper-

mica, which is another like it, made chiefly
of copper; and this foliated iron is called
"micaceous iron." You have then these
two great orders, Needle-crystals, made
(probably) of grains in rows; and Leaf-
. crystals, made (probably) of needles inter-
woven; now, lastly, there are crystals of a
third order, in heaps, or knots, or masses,
which may be made either of leaves laid
one upon another, or of needles bound like
Roman fasces; and mica itself, when it is
well crystallized, puts itself into such masses,
as if to show us how others are made. Here
is a brown six-sided crystal, quite as beautifully chiseled at the sides as any castle
tower, but you see it is entirely built of
folia of mica, one laid above another, which
break away the moment I touch the edge
with my knife. Now, here is another hexagonal tower, of just the same size and
color, which I want you to compare with
the mica carefully; but as I cannot wait for
you to do it just now, I must tell you quickly what main differences to look for. First,
you will feel it far heavier than the mica.
Then, though its surface looks quite micaceous in the folia of it when you try them
with the knife, you will find you cannot
break them away——

KATHLEEN. May I try?

L. Yes, you mistrusting Katie. Here's
my strong knife for you. (*Experimental
pause.* KATHLEEN *doing her best.*) You'll

have that knife shutting on your finger
presently, Kate; and I don't know a girl
who would like less to have her hand tied
up for a week.

KATHLEEN (*who also does not like to be
beaten—giving up the knife despondently*).
What *can* the nasty hard thing be?

L. It is nothing but indurated clay, Kate :
very hard set certainly, yet not so hard as
it might be. If it were thoroughly well
crystallized, you would see none of those
micaceous fractures ; and the stone would
be quite red and clear, all through.

KATHLEEN. Oh, cannot you show us one?

L. Egypt can, if you ask her; she has a beautiful one in the clasp of her favorite bracelet.

KATHLEEN. Why, that's a ruby !

L. Well, so is that thing you've been
scratching at.

KATHLEEN. My goodness !

(*Takes up the stone again, very delicately ;
and drops it. General consternation.*)

L. Never mind, Katie ; you might drop it
from the top of the house, and do it no
harm. But though you really are a very
good girl, and as good-natured as anybody
can possibly be, remember, you have your
faults, like other people ; and, if I were you,
the next time I wanted to assert anything
energetically, I would assert it by " my
badness," not " my goodness."

KATHLEEN. Ah, now it's too bad of you !

L. Well, then, I'll invoke, on occasion,

my " too-badness." But you may as well pick up the ruby, now you have dropped it ; and look carefully at the beautiful hexagonal lines which gleam on its surface ; and here is a pretty white sapphire (essentially the same stone as the ruby), in which you will see the same lovely structure, like the threads of the finest white cobweb. I do not know what is the exact method of a ruby's construction ; but you see by these lines, what fine construction there *is*, even in this hardest of stones (after the diamond), which usually appears as a massive lump or knot. There is therefore no real mineralogical distinction between needle crystals, and knotted crystals, but practically, crystallized masses throw themselves into one of the three groups we have been examining to-day ; and appear either as Needles, as Folia, or as Knots ; when they are in needles (or fibers), they make the stones or rocks formed out of then " *fibrous ;*" when they are in folia, they make them " *foliated ;*" when they are in knots (or grains), " *granular.*" Fibrous rocks are comparatively rare, in mass ; but fibrous minerals are innumerable : and it is often a question which really no one but a young lady could possibly settle, whether one should call the fibers composing them " threads " or " needles." Here is amianthus, for instance, which is quite as fine and soft as any cotton thread you ever sewed with.; and here is sulphide of bismuth, with

6

sharper points and brighter luster than your
finest needles have ; and fastened in white
webs of quartz more delicate than your finest
lace ; and here is sulphide of antimony, which
looks like mere purple wool, but it is all of
purple needle crystals, and here is red oxide
of copper (you must not breathe on it as
you look, or you may blow some of the films
of it off the stone), which is simply a woven
tissue of scarlet silk.   However, these finer
thread-forms are comparatively rare, while
the bolder and needle-like crystals occur
constantly ; so that, I believe, " Needle-
crystal " is the best word (the grand one is
"Acicular" crystal, but Sibyl will tell you it is
all the same, only less easily understood ; and
therefore more scientific).   Then the Leaf-
crystals, as I said, form an immense mass
of foliated rocks ; and the Granular crystals,
which are of many kinds, form essentially
granular, or granitic and porphyritic rocks ;
and it is always a point of more interest to
me (and I think will ultimately be to you),
to consider the causes which force a given
mineral to take any one of these three general
forms, than what the · peculiar geometrical
limitations are, belonging to its own crystals.*   It is more interesting to me, for
instance, to try and find out why the red
oxide of copper, usually crystallizing in
cubes or octahedrons, makes itself exquisite-

* Note iv.

ly, out of its cubes, into this red silk in one particular Cornish mine, than what are the absolutely necessary angles of the octahedron, which is its common form. At all events, that mathematical part of crystallography is quite beyond girls' strength ; but these questions of the various tempers and manners of crystals are not only comprehensible by you, but full of the most curious teaching for you. For in the fulfillment, to the best of their power, of their adopted form under given circumstances there are conditions entirely resembling those of human virtue : and indeed expressible under no term so proper as that of the Virtue, or Courage of crystals :—which, if you are not afraid of the crystals making you ashamed of yourselves, we will try to get some notion of, to-morrow. But it will be a bye-lecture, and more about yourselves than the minerals. Don't come unless you like.

MARY. I'm sure the crystals will make us ashamed of ourselves ; but we'll come, for all that.

L. Meantime, look well and quietly over these needle, or thread crystals, and those on the other two tables, with magnifying glasses ; and see what thoughts will come into your little heads about them. For the best thoughts are generally those which come without being forced, one does not know how. And so I hope you will get through your wet day patiently.

LECTURE 5
CRYSTAL VIRTUES.

LECTURE V.

CRYSTAL VIRTUES.

A quiet talk, in the afternoon, by the sunniest window of the Drawing-room. Present, FLORRIE, ISABEL, MAY, LUCILLA, KATHLEEN, DORA, MARY, *and some others, who have saved time for the bye-Lecture.*

L. So you have really come, like good girls, to be made ashamed of yourselves?

DORA (*very meekly*). No, we needn't be made so; we always are.

L. Well, I believe that's truer than most pretty speeches : but you know, you saucy girl, some people have more reason to be so than others.   Are you sure everybody is, as well as you?

THE GENERAL VOICE. Yes, yes; everybody.

L. What! Florrie ashamed of herself?

(FLORRIE *hides behind the curtain.*)

L. And Isabel?

(ISABEL *hides under the table.*)

L. And May?

(MAY *runs into the corner behind the piano.*)

L. And Lucilla?

(LUCILLA *hides her face in her hands.*)

87

L. Dear, dear; but this will never do. I
shall have to tell you of the faults of the
crystals, instead of virtues, to put you in
heart again.

May (*coming out of her corner*). Oh!
have the crystals faults, like us?

L. Certainly, May. Their best virtues
are shown in fighting their faults; and some
have a great many faults; and some are
very naughty crystals indeed.

Florrie (*from behind her curtain*). As
naughty as me?

Isabel (*peeping out from under the table-
cloth*). Or me?

L. Well, I don't know. They never forget their syntax, children, when once they've
been taught it. But I think some of them
are, on the whole, worse than any of you.
Not that it's amiable of you to look so radi-
ant, all in a minute, on that account.

Dora. Oh! but it's so much more comfortable.

(*Everybody seems to recover their spirits.
Eclipse of* Florrie *and* Isabel *terminates.*)

L. What kindly creatures girls are, after
all, to their neighbors' failings! I think you
may be ashamed of yourselves indeed, now,
children! I can tell you, you shall hear of
the highest crystalline merits that I can
think of, to-day: and I wish there were
more of them; but crystals have a limited,
though a stern, code of morals; and their
essential virtues are but two;—the first is

to be pure, and the second to be well shaped.

MARY. Pure! Does that mean clear—transparent?

L. No; unless in the case of a transparent substance. You cannot have a transparent crystal of gold; but you may have a perfectly pure one.

ISABEL. But you said it was the shape that made things be crystals; therefore, oughtn't their shape to be their first virtue, not their second?

L. Right, you troublesome mousie. But I call their shape only their second virtue, because it depends on time and accident, and things which the crystal cannot help. If it is cooled too quickly, or shaken, it must take what shape it can; but it seems as if, even then, it had in itself the power of rejecting impurity, if it has crystalline life enough. Here is a crystal of quartz, well enough shaped in its way; but it seems to have been languid and sick at heart; and some white milky substance has got into it, and mixed itself up with it, all through. It makes the quartz quiet yellow, if you hold it up to the light, and milky blue on the surface. Here is another, broken into a thousand separate facets and out of all traceable shape; but as pure as a mountain spring. I like this one best.

THE AUDIENCE. So do I—and I—and I.

MARY. Would a crystallographer?

L. I think so. He would find many more laws curiously exemplified in the irregularly ground but pure crystal. But it is a futile question, this of first or second. Purity is in most cases a prior, if not a nobler, virtue; at all events it is most convenient to think about it first.

MARY. But what ought we to think about it? Is there much to be thought—I mean, much to puzzle one?

L. I don't know what you call "much." It is a long time since I met with anything in which there was little. There's not much in this, perhaps. The crystal must be either dirty or clean,—and there's an end. So it is with one's hands, and with one's heart— only you can wash your hands without changing them, but not hearts, nor crystals. On the whole, while you are young, it will be as well to take care that your hearts don't want much washing; for they may perhaps need wringing also, when they do.

(*Audience doubtful and uncomfortable.* LUCILLA *at last takes courage.*)

LUCILLA. Oh! but surely, sir, we cannot make our hearts clean?

L. Not easily, Lucilla; so you had better keep them so, when they are.

LUCILLA. When they are! But, sir—

L. Well?

LUCILLA. Sir—surely—are we not told that they are all evil?

L. Wait a little, Lucilla; that is difficult ground you are getting upon and we must keep to our crystals, till at least we understand what *their* good and evil consist in; they may help us afterwards to some useful hints about our own. I said that their goodness consisted chiefly in purity of substance, and perfectness of form : but those are rather the *effects* of their goodness, than the goodness itself. The inherent virtues of the crystals, resulting in these outer conditions, might really seem to be best described in the words we should use respecting living creatures—"force of heart" and "steadiness of purpose." There seem to be in some crystals, from the beginning, an unconquerable purity of vital power, and strength of crystal spirit. Whatever dead substance, unacceptant of this energy, comes in their way, is either rejected, or forced to take some beautiful subordinate form ; the purity of the crystal remains unsullied, and every atom of it bright with coherent energy. Then the second condition is, that from the beginning of its whole structure, a fine crystal seems to have determined that it will be of a certain size and of a certain shape ; it persists in this plan, and completes it. Here is a perfect crystal of quartz for you. It is of an unusual form, and one which it might seem very difficult to build—a pyramid with convex sides, composed of other minor pyramids. But there

is not a flaw in its contour throughout ; **not**
one of its myriads of component sides but is
as bright as a jeweler's faceted work (and
far finer, if you saw it close).   The crystal
points are as sharp as javelins ; their edges
will cut glass with a touch.   Anything more
resolute, consummate, determinate in form,
cannot be conceived.   Here, on the other
hand, is a crystal of the same substance, in
a perfectly simple type of form—a plain six-
sided prism ; but from its base to its point,
—and it is nine inches long,—it has never
for one instant made up its mind what thickness it will have.   It seems to have begun
by making itself as thick as it thought possible with the quantity of material at command.   Still not being as thick as it would
like to be, it has clumsily glued on more
substance at one of its sides.   Then it has
thinned itself, in a panic of economy ; then
puffed itself out again ; then starved one side
to enlarge another ; then warped itself quite
out of its first line.   Opaque, rough-surfaced,
jagged on the edge, distorted in the spine,
it exhibits a quite human image of decrepi-
tude and dishonor ; but the worst of all the
signs of its decay and helplessness, is that
half-way up, a parasite crystal, smaller,
but just as sickly, has rooted itself in the
side of the larger one, eating out a cavity
round its root, and then growing backwards,
or downwards, contrary to the direction of
the main crystal.   Yet I cannot trace the

least difference in purity of substance between the first most noble stone, and this ignoble and dissolute one. The impurity of the last is in its will, or want of will.

MARY. Oh, if we could but understand the the meaning of it all !

L. We can understand all that is good for us. It is just as true for us, as for the crystal, that the nobleness of life depends on its consistency,—clearness of purpose,—quiet and ceaseless energy. All doubt, and repenting, and botching, and re-touching, and wondering what will it be best to do next, are vice, as well as misery.

MARY (*much wondering*). But must not one repent when one does wrong, and hesitate when one can't see one's way?

L. You have no business at all to do wrong; nor to get into any way that you cannot see. Your intelligence should always be far in advance of your act. Whenever you do not know what you are about, you are sure to be doing wrong.

KATHLEEN. Oh, dear, but I never know what I am about !

L. Very true, Katie, but it is a great deal to know, if you know that. And you find that you have done wrong afterwards ; and perhaps some day you may begin to know. or at least, think, what you are about.

ISABEL. But surely people can't do very wrong if they don't know, can they? I mean, they can't be very naughty. They

can be wrong, like Kathleen or me, when
we make mistakes; but not wrong in the
dreadful way. I can't express what I
mean; but there are two sorts of wrong,
are there not?

L. Yes, Isabel; but you will find that the
great difference is between kind and unkind
wrongs, not between meant and unmeant
wrong. Very few people really mean to do
wrong,—in a deep sense, none. They only
don't know what they are about. Cain did
not mean to do wrong when he killed Abel.

(ISABEL *draws a deep breath, and opens
her eyes very wide.*)

L. No, Isabel; and there are countless
Cains among us now, who kill their brothers
by the score a day, not only for less provo-
cation than Cain had, but for *no* provoca-
tion,—and merely for what they can make
of their bones,—yet do not think they are
doing wrong in the least. Then sometimes
you have the business reversed, as over in
America these last years, where you have
seen Abel resolutely killing Cain, and not
thinking he is doing wrong. The great difficulty is always to open people's eyes: to
touch their feelings, and break their hearts,
is easy; the difficult thing is to break their
heads. What does it matter, as long as they
remain stupid, whether you change their
feelings or not? You cannot be always at
their elbow to tell them what is right: and
they may just do as wrong as before, or

worse ; and their best intentions merely make the road smooth for them,—you know where, children. For it is not the place itself that is paved with them, as people say so often. You can't pave the bottomless pit ; but you may the road to it.

MAY. Well, but if people do as well as they can see how, surely that is the right for them, isn't it ?

L. No, May, not a bit of it ; right is right, and wrong is wrong. It is only the fool who does wrong, and says he "did it for the best." And if there's one sort of person in the world that the Bible speaks harder of than another, it is fools. Their particular and chief way of saying "There is no God" is this, of declaring that whatever their "public opinion" may be, is right : and that God's opinion is of no consequence.

MAY. But surely nobody can always know what is right?

L. Yes, you always can, for to-day ; and if you do what you see of it to-day, you will see more of it, and more clearly, to-morrow. Here for instance, you children are at school, and have to learn French, and arithmetic, and music, and several other such things. That is your "right" for the present ; the "right" for us, your teachers, is to see that you learn as much as you can without spoiling your dinner, your sleep, or your play ; and that what you do learn, you learn well. You all know when you learn with a will, and when you dawdle. There's no doubt of conscience about that, I suppose?

VIOLET. No; but if one wants to read an amusing book, instead of learning one's lesson?

L. You don't call that a, "question," seriously, Violet? You are then merely deciding whether you will resolutely do wrong or not.

MARY. But in after life, how many fearful difficulties may arise, however one tries to know or to do what is right!

L. You are much too sensible a girl, Mary, to have felt that, whatever you may have seen. A great many of young ladies' difficulties arise from their falling in love with a wrong person; but they have no business to let themselves fall in love, till they know he is the right one.

DORA. How many thousands ought he to have a year?

L. (*disdaining reply*). There are, of course, certain crises of fortune when one has to take care of oneself, and mind shrewdly what one is about. There is never any real doubt about the path, but you may have to walk very slowly.

MARY. And if one is forced to do a wrong thing by some one who has authority over you?

L. My dear, no one can be forced to do a wrong thing, for the guilt is in the will: but you may any day be forced to do a fatal thing, as you might be forced to take poison; the remarkable law of nature in such cases being, that it is always unfortunate *you* who are poisoned, and not the person who gives you the dose. It is a very strange law, but it *is* a law. Nature merely sees to the carrying out of the normal operation of arsenic. She never troubles herself to ask who gave it you. So also you may be starved to death, morally as well as physically, by other people's faults. You are, on the whole, very good children sitting here to-day; do you think that your goodness comes all by your own contriving? or that you are gentle and kind because your dispositions are naturally more angelic than those of the poor girls who are playing, with wild eyes, on the dust-heaps in the alleys of our great towns; and who will one day fill their prisons,—or, better, their graves? Heaven only knows where they, and we who have cast them there, shall stand at last. But the main judgment question will be, I suppose, for all of us, "Did you keep a good heart through it?" What you were, others may answer for;—what you tried to be, you must answer for yourself. Was the heart pure and true—tell us that?

And so we come back to your sorrowful question, Lucilla, which I put aside a little ago. You would be afraid to answer that **your heart** *was* **pure and true, would not you?**

LUCILLA. Yes, indeed, sir.

L. Because you have been taught that it is all evil—"only evil continually." Somehow, often as people say that, they never seem, to me, to believe it. Do you really believe it?

LUCILLA. Yes, sir; I hope so.

L. That you have an entirely bad heart?

LUCILLA (*a little uncomfortable at the substitution of the monosyllable for the dissyllable, nevertheless persisting in her orthodoxy*). Yes, sir.

L. Florrie, I am sure you are tired; I never like you to stay when you are tired; but, you know, you must not play with the kitten while we're talking.

FLORRIE. Oh! but I'm not tired; and I'm only nursing her. She'll be asleep in my lap, directly.

L. Stop! that puts me in mind of something I had to show you, about minerals that are like hair. I want a hair out of Tittie's tail.

FLORRIE (*quite rude, in her surprise, even to the point of repeating expressions*). Out of Tittie's tail!

L. Yes: a brown one: Lucilla, you can get at the tip of it nicely, under Florrie's arm; just pull one out for me.

LUCILLA. Oh! but, sir, it will hurt her so!

L. Never mind; she can't scratch you while Florrie is holding her. Now that I think of it, you had better pull out two.

LUCILLA. But then she may scratch Florrie! and it will hurt her so, sir! if you only want brown hairs, wouldn't two of mine do?

L. Would you really rather pull out your own than Tittie's?

LUCILLA. Oh, of course, if mine will do.

L. But that's very wicked, Lucilla!

LUCILLA. Wicked, sir?

L. Yes; if your heart was not so bad, you would much rather pull all the cat's hairs out than one of your own.

LUCILLA. Oh! but, sir, I didn't mean bad like that.

L. I believe, if the truth were told, Lucilla, you would like to tie a kettle to Tittie's tail, and hunt her round the playground.

LUCILLA. Indeed, I should not, sir.

L. That's not true, Lucilla; you know it cannot be.

LUCILLA. Sir?

L. Certainly it is not;—how can you possibly speak any truth out of such a heart as you have? It is wholly deceitful.

LUCILLA. Oh! no, no; I don't mean that way; I don't mean that it makes me tell lies, quite out.

L. Only that it tells lies within you?

LUCILLA. Yes.

L. Then, outside of it, you know what is true, and say so; and I may trust the outside of your heart; but within, it is all foul and false. Is that the way?

Lucilla. I suppose so : I don't understand it quite.

L. There is no occasion for understanding
it ; but do you feel it ? Are you sure that
your heart is deceitful above all things, and
desperately wicked?

Lucilla. (*much relieved by finding herself
among phrases with which she is acquainted*).
Yes, sir. I'm sure of that.

L. (*pensively*). I'm sorry for it, Lucilla.

Lucilla. So am I, indeed.

L.   What are you sorry with, Lucilla?

Lucilla. Sorry with, sir?

L.   Yes ; I mean, where do you feel sorry,
in your feet?

Lucilla (*laughing a little*).   No, sir, of
course.

L. In your shoulders, then?

Lucilla. No, sir.

L. You are sure of that ?   Because, I
fear, sorrow in the shoulders would not be
worth much.

Lucilla. I suppose I feel it in my heart,
if I really am sorry.

L. If you really are ! Do you mean to
say that you are sure you are utterly wicked,
and yet to do not care?

Lucilla. No, indeed ; I have cried about
it often.

L. Well, then, you are sorry in your
heart?

Lucilla. Yes, when the sorrow is worth
anything.

L. Even if it be not, it cannot be anywhere else but there. It is not the crystalline lens of your eyes which is sorry, when
you cry?

LUCILLA. No, sir, of course.

L. Then, have you two hearts; one of
which is wicked, and the other grieved? or
is one side of it sorry for the other side?

LUCILLA (*weary of cross-examination, and
a little vexed*). Indeed, sir, you know I can't
understand it; but you know how it is written—"another law in my members, war-
ring against the law of my mind."

L. Yes, Lucilla, I know how it is written;
but I do not see that it will help us to know
that, if we neither understand what is written, nor feel it. And you will not get nearer
to the meaning of one verse, if, as soon as
you are puzzled by it, you escape to another,
introducing three new words—"law,"
"members," and "mind"; not one of which
you at present know the meaning of; and
respecting which, you probably never will
be much wiser; since men like Montesquieu
and Locke have spent great part of their
lives in endeavoring to explain two of them.

LUCILLA. Oh! please, sir, ask somebody
else.

L. If I thought any one else could answer
better than you, Lucilla, I would: but suppose I try, instead, myself, to explain your
feelings to you?

LUCILLA. Oh, yes; please do.

L. Mind, I say your "feelings," not your "belief." For I cannot undertake to explain anybody's beliefs. Still I must try a little first, to explain the belief also, because I want to draw it to some issue. As far as I understand what you say, or any one else, taught as you have been taught, says, on this matter,—you think that there is an external goodness, a whited-sepulcher kind of goodness, which appears beautiful outwardly, but is within full of uncleanness : a deep secret guilt, of which we ourselves are not sensible ; and which can only be seen by the Maker of us all. (*Approving murmurs from audience.*)

L. Is it not so with the body as well as the soul ?

(*Looked notes of interrogation.*)

L. A skull, for instance, is not a beautiful thing ?

(*Grave faces, signifying " Certainly not, " and " What next ? "*)

L. And if you all could see in each other with clear eyes, whatever God sees beneath those fair faces of yours, you would not like it ?

(*Murmured No's.*)

L. Nor would it be good for you?

(*Silence.*)

L. The probability being that what God does not allow you to see, He does not wish you to see ; nor even to think of?

(*Silence prolonged.*)

L. It would not at all be good for you, for instance, whenever you were washing your faces, and braiding your hair, to be thinking of the shapes of the jawbones, and of the cartilage of the nose, and of the jagged sutures of the scalp?

(*Resolutely whispered No's.*)

L. Still less to see through a clear glass the daily processes of nourishment and decay?

(*No's.*)

L. Still less if instead of merely inferior and preparatory conditions of structure, as in the skeleton,—or inferior offices of structure, as in operations of life and death,—there were actual disease in the body; ghastly and dreadful. You would try to cure it; but having taken such measures as were necessary, you would not think the cure likely to be promoted by perpetually watching the wounds, or thinking of them. On the contrary, you would be thankful for every moment of forgetfulness; as, in daily health, you must be thankful that your Maker has veiled whatever is fearful in your frame under a sweet and manifest beauty; and has made it your duty, and your only safety, to rejoice in that, both in yourself and in others :—not indeed concealing, or refusing to believe in sickness, if it come; but never dwelling on it.

Now, your wisdom and duty touching **soul-sickness are just the same.** Ascertain clearly what is wrong with you ; and so far as you know any means of mending it, take those means, and have done ; when you are examining yourself, never call yourself merely a "sinner," that is very cheap abuse ; and utterly useless. You may even get to like it, and be proud of it. But call yourself a liar, a coward, a sluggard, a glutton, or an evil-eyed, jealous wretch, if you indeed find yourself to be in any wise any of these. Take steady means to check yourself in whatever fault you have ascertained, and justly accused yourself of. And as soon as you are in active way of mending, you will be no more inclined to moan over an undefined corruption. For the rest, you will find it less easy to uproot faults, than to choke them by gaining virtues. Do not think of your faults ; still less of others' faults : in every person who comes near you, look for what is good and strong : honor that ; rejoice in it ; and, as you can, try to imitate it ; and your faults will drop off like dead leaves, when their time comes. If, on looking back, your whole life should seem rugged as a palm-tree stem ; still, never mind, so long as it had been growing ; and has its grand green shade of leaves, and weight of honeyed fruit at top. And even if you cannot find much good in yourself at last, think that it does not much matter to the universe either what you were, or are ; think how many people are noble, if you cannot be ; and rejoice in *their* nobleness. An immense quantity of modern confession of sin, even when honest, is merely a sickly egotism ; which will rather gloat over its own evil, than lose the centralization of its interest in itself.

MARY. But then, if we ought to forget ourselves so much, how did the old Greek proverb "Know thyself" come to be so highly estemed?

L. My dear, it is the proverb of proverbs ; Apollo's proverb, and the sun's—but do you think you can know yourself by looking *into* yourself? Never. You can know what you are, only by looking *out* of yourself. Measure your own powers with those of others ; compare your own interests with those of others ; try to understand what you appear to them, as well as what they appear to you ; and judge of yourselves, in all things, relatively and subordinately ; not positively : starting always with a wholesome conviction of the probability that there is nothing particular about you. For instance, some of you perhaps think you can write poetry. Dwell on your own feelings ; and doings :—and you will soon think yourselves Tenth Muses ; but forget your own feelings ; and try, instead, to understand a line or two of Chaucer or Dante : and you will soon begin to feel yourselves very foolish girls—which is much like the fact. •

So, something which befalls you **may**

seem a great misfortune ;—you meditate
over its effects on you personally ; and begin
to think that it is a chastisement, or a warning, or a this or that or the other of profound
significance ; and that all the angels in
heaven have left their business for a little
while, that they may watch its effects on
your mind.   But give up this egotistic indulgence of your fancy; examine a little
what misfortunes, greater a thousand fold,
are happening, every second, to twenty
times worthier persons : and your self-con-
sciousness will change into pity and humility ; and you will know yourself, so far as
to understand that " there hath nothing
taken thee but what is common to man."

Now, Lucilla, these are the practical con-
clusions which any person of sense would
arrive at, supposing the texts which relate
to the inner evil of the heart were as many,
and as prominent, as they are often supposed to be by careless readers.   But the
way in which common people read their
Bibles is just like the way that the old monks
thought hedgehogs ate grapes.   They rolled
themselves (it was said), over and over,
where the grapes lay on the ground.   What
fruit stuck to their spines, they carried off,
and ate.   So your hedgehoggy readers roll
themselves over and over their Bibles, and
declare that whatever sticks to their own
spines is Scripture, and that nothing else
is.   But you can only get the skins of the

texts that way. If you want their juice,
you must press them in cluster. Now, the
clustered texts about the human heart, insist,
as a body, not on any inherent corruption
in all hearts, but on the terrific distinction
between the bad and the good ones. "A
good man, out of the good treasure of his
heart, bringeth forth that which is good;
and an evil man, out of the evil treasure,
bringeth forth that which is evil." "They
on the rock are they which, in an honest
and good heart, having heard the word,
keep it." "Delight thyself in the Lord, and
He shall give thee the desires of thine
heart." "The wicked have bent their bow,
that they may privily shoot at him that is
upright in heart," And so on; they are
countless, to the same effect. And, for all
of us, the question is not at all to ascertain
how much or how little corruption there is
in human nature; but to ascertain whether,
out of all the mass of that nature, we are of
the sheep or the goat breed; whether we
are people of upright heart, being shot at, or
people of crooked heart, shooting. And, of
all the texts bearing on the subject, this,
which is a quite simple and practical order,
is the one you have chiefly to hold in mind.
"Keep thy heart with all diligence, for out
of it are the issues of life."

LUCILLA. And yet, how inconsistent the
texts seem!

L. Nonsense, Lucilla! do you think the

universe is bound to look consistent to a girl
of fifteen? Look up at your own room
window;—you can just see it from where
you sit. I'm glad that it is left open, as it
ought to be, in so fine a day. But do you
see what a black spot it looks, in the sun-
lighted wall?

Lucilla. Yes, it looks as black as ink.

L. Yet you know it is a very bright room
when you are inside of it; quite as bright
as there is any occasion for it to be, that its
little lady may see to keep it tidy. Well, it
is very probable, also, that if you could look
into your heart from the sun's point of view,
it might appear a very black hole indeed:
nay, the sun may sometimes think good to
tell you that it looks so to Him; but He will
come into it, and make it very cheerful for
you, for all that, if you don't put the shutters
up. And the one question for *you*, remember, is not "dark or light?" but "tidy or
untidy?" Look well to your sweeping and
garnishing; and be sure it is only the ban-
ished spirit, or some of the seven wickeder
ones at his back, who will still whisper to
you that it is all black.

CRYSTAL QUARRELS.

LECTURE VI.

CRYSTAL QUARRELS.

Full conclave, in Schoolroom. There has been a game of crystallization in the morning, of which various account has to be rendered. In particular, everybody has to explain why they were always where they were not intended to be.

L. (*having received and considered the reported.*) You have got on pretty well, children : but you know these were easy figures you have been trying. Wait till I have drawn you out the plans of some crystals of snow !

MARY. I don't think those will be the most difficult :—they are so beautiful that we shall remember our places better ; and then they are all regular, and in stars : it is those twisty oblique ones we are afraid of.

L. Read Carlyle's account of the battle of Leuthen, and learn Friedrich's " oblique order." You will "get it done for once, I think, provided you *can* march as a pair of compasses would." But remember, when you can construct the most difficult single figures, you have only learned half the game

III

—nothing so much as the half, indeed, as the crystals themselves play it.

MARY. Indeed ; what else is there ?

L. It is seldom that any mineral crystallizes alone. Usually two or three, under quite different crystalline laws, form together. They do this absolutely without flaw or fault, when they are in fine temper : and observe what this signifies. It signifies that the two, or more, minerals of different natures agree, somehow between themselves, how much space each will want ;— agree which of them shall give way to the other at their junction ; or in what measure each will accommodate itself to the other's shape ! And then each takes its permitted shape, and allotted share of space ; yielding, or being yielded to, as it builds till each crystal has fitted itself perfectly and gracefully to its differently-natured neighbor. So that, in order to practice this, in even the simplest terms, you must divide into two parties, wearing different colors ; each must choose a different figure to construct ; and you must form one of these figures through the other, both going on at the same time.

MARY. I think *we* may perhaps manage it ; but I cannot at all understand how the crystals do. It seems to imply so much preconcerting of plan, and so much giving way to each other, as if they really were living.

L. Yes, it implies both the concurrence and compromise, regulating all willfulness of design : and, more curious still, the crystals do *not* always give way to each other. They show exactly the same varieties of temper that human creatures might. Sometimes they yield the required place with perfect grace and courtesy ; forming fantastic, but exquisitely finished groups : and sometimes they will not yield at all ; but fight furiously for their places, losing all shape and honor, and even their own likeness, in the contest.

MARY. But is not that wholly wonderful ? How is it that one never sees it spoken of in books ?

L. The scientific men are all busy in determining the constant laws under which the struggle takes place; these indefinite humors of the elements are of no interest to them. And unscientific people rarely give themselves the trouble of thinking at all, when they look at stones. Not that it is of much use to think ; the more one thinks, the more one is puzzled.

MARY. Surely it is more wonderful than anything in botany ?

L. Everything has its own wonders ; but, given the nature of the plant, it is easier to understand what a flower will do, and why it does it, than, given anything we as yet know of stone-nature, to understand what a crystal will do, and why it does it. You at

8

once admit a kind of volition and choice, in
the flower; but we are not accustomed to
attribute anything of the kind to the crystal.
Yet there is, in reality, more likeness to
some conditions of human feeling among
stones than among plants. There is a far
greater difference between kindly-tempered
and ill-tempered crystals of the same mineral, than between any two specimens of the
same flower: and the friendships and wars
of crystals depend more definitely and curiously on their varieties of disposition, than
any associations of flowers. Here, for instance, is a good garnet, living with good
mica; one rich red, and the other silver
white; the mica leaves exactly room enough
for the garnet to crystallize comfortably in;
and the garnet lives happily in its little
white house; fitted to it, like a pholas in
its cell. But here are wicked garnets living
with wicked mica. See what ruin they
make of each other! You cannot tell which
is which; the garnets look like dull red stains
on the crumbling stones. By the way, I
never could understand, if St. Gothard is a
real saint, why he can't keep his garnets in
better order. These are all under his care;
but I suppose there are too many of them
for him to look after. The streets of Airolo
are paved with them.

MAY. Paved with garnets?

L. With mica-slate and garnets; I broke
this bit out of a paving stone. Now garnets

and mica are natural friends, and generally
fond of each other; but you see how they
quarrel when they are ill brought up. So it
is always. Good crystals are friendly with
almost all other good crystals, however little
they chance to see of each other, or however opposite their habits may be; while
wicked crystals quarrel with one another,
though they may be exactly alike in habits,
and see each other continually. And of
course the wicked crystals quarrel with the
good ones.

ISABEL. Then do the good ones get angry?

L. No, never: they attend to their own
work and life; and live it as well as they
can, though they are always the sufferers.
Here, for instance, is a rock crystal of the
purest race and finest temper, who was born,
unhappily for him, in a bad neighborhood,
near Beaufort in Savoy; and he has had to
fight with vile calcareous mud all his life.
See here, when he was but a child, it came
down on him, and nearly buried him; a
weaker crystal would have died in despair;
but he only gathered himself together, like
Hercules against the serpents, and threw a
layer of crystal over the clay; conquered
it,—imprisoned it,—and lived on. Then,
when he was a little older, came more clay;
and poured itself upon him here, at the side;
and he has laid crystal over that, and lived
on, in his purity. Then the clay came on

at his angles, and tried to cover them, and
round them away; but upon that he threw
out buttress-crystals at his angles, all as true
to his own central line as chapels round a
cathedral apse; and clustered them round
the clay; and conquered it again. At last
the clay came on at his summit, and tried
to blunt his summit; but he could not en-
dure that for an instant; and left his flanks
all rough, but pure; and fought the clay at
his crest, and built crest over crest and peak
over peak, till the clay surrendered at last,
änd here is his summit, smooth and pure,
terminating a pyramid of alternate clay and
crystal, half a foot high!

LILY. Oh, how nice of him! What a
dear, brave crystal! But I can't bear to see
his flanks all broken, and the clay within
them.

L. Yes; it was an evil chance for him,
the being born to such contention; there are
some enemies so base that even to hold them
captive is a kind of dishonor. But look,
here has been quite a different kind of struggle: the adverse power has been more
orderly, and has fought the pure crystal in
ranks as firm as its own. This is not mere
rage and impediment of crowded evil: here
is a disciplined hostility; army against army.

LILY. Oh, but this is much more beautiful!

L. Yes, for both the elements have true
virtue in them; it is a pity they are at war,
but they war grandly.

MARY. But is this the same clay as in the other crystal?

L. I used the word clay for shortness. In both, the enemy is really limestone; but in the first, disordered, and mixed with true clay; while, here, it is nearly pure and crystallizes into its own primitive form, the oblique six-sided one, which you know: and out of these it makes regiments; and then squares of the regiments, and so charges the rock crystal, literally in square against column.

ISABEL. Please, please, let me see. And what does the rock crystal do?

L. The rock crystal seems able to do nothing. The calcite cuts it through at every charge. Look here,—and here! The loveliest crystal in the whole group is hewn fairly into two pieces.

ISABEL. Oh, dear; but is the calcite harder than the crystal then?

L. No, softer. Very much softer.

MARY. But then, how can it possibly cut the crystal?

L. It did not really cut it, though it passes through it. The two were formed together, as I told you; but no one knows how. Still, it is strange that this hard quartz has in all cases a good-natured way with it, of yielding to everything else. All sorts of soft things make nests for themselves in it; and it never makes a nest for itself in anything. It has all the rough outside work;

and every sort of cowardly and weak mineral can shelter itself within it. Look ; these are hexagonal plates of mica ; if they were out-side of this crystal they would break, like burnt paper ; but they are inside of it,— nothing can hurt them,—the crystal has taken them into its very heart, keeping all their delicate edges as sharp as if they were under water, instead of bathed in rock. Here is a piece of branched silver : you can bend it with a touch of your finger, but the stamp of its every fiber is on the rock in which it lay, as if the quartz had been as soft as wool.

LILY. Oh, the good, good quartz ! But does it never get inside of anything ?

L. As it is a little Irish girl who asks, I may perhaps answer, without being laughed at, that it gets inside of itself sometimes. But I don't remember seeing quartz make a nest for itself in anything else.

ISABEL. Please, there was something I heard you talking about, last time, with Miss Mary. I was at my lessons, but I heard something about nests ; and I thought it was birds' nests ; and I couldn't help listen-ing ; and then, I remember, it was about "nests of quartz in granite." I remember, because I was so disappointed !

L. Yes, mousie, you remember quite rightly ; but I can't tell you about those nests to-day, nor perhaps to-morrow ; but there's no contradiction between my saying

then, and now ; I will show you that there
is not, some day. Will you trust me mean-
while ?

ISABEL. Won't I !

L. Well, then, look, lastly, at this piece
of courtesy in quartz ; it is on a small scale,
but wonderfully pretty. Here is nobly born
quartz living with a green mineral, called
epidote ; and they are immense friends.
Now, you see, a comparatively large and
strong quartz-crystal, and a very weak and
slender little one of epidote, have begun to
grow, close by each other, and sloping un-
luckily towards each other, so that at last
they meet. They cannot go on growing
together ; the quartz crystal is five times as
thick, and more than twenty times as
strong,* as the epidote ; but he stops at once,
just in the very crowning moment of his life,
when he is building his own summit ! He
lets the pale little film of epidote grow right
past him ; stopping his own summit for it ;
and he never himself grows any more.

LILY (*after some silence of wonder*). But
is the quartz *never* wicked then ?

L. Yes, but the wickedest quartz seems
good-natured, compared to other things.
Here are two very characteristic examples ;
one is good quartz, living with good pearl-
spar, and the other, wicked quartz, living

* Quartz is not much harder than epidote ; the
strength is only supposed to be in some proportion to
the squares of the diameters.

with wicked pearl-spar. In both, the quartz yields to the soft carbonate of iron : but, in the first place, the iron takes only what it needs of room; and is inserted into the planes of the rock crystal with such precision that you must break it away before you can tell whether it really penetrates the quartz or not ; while the crystals of iron are perfectly formed, and have a lovely bloom on their surface besides.   But, here, when the two minerals quarrel, the unhappy quartz has all its surface jagged and torn to pieces, and there is not a single iron crystal whose shape you can completely trace. But the quartz has the worst of it, in both instances.

VIOLET. Might we look at that piece of broken quartz again, with the weak little film across it ? it seems such a strange lovely thing, like the self-sacrifice of a human being.

L. The self-sacrifice of a human being is not a lovely thing, Violet.   It is often a necessary and noble thing ; but no form nor degree of suicide can be ever lovely.

VIOLET. But self-sacrifice is not suicide !

L. What is it then ?

VIOLET. Giving up one's self for another.

L. Well ; and what do you mean by "giving up one's self"?

VIOLET. Giving up one's tastes, one's feelings, one's time, one's happiness, and so on, to make others happy.

L. I hope you will never marry anybody,

Violet, who expects you to make him happy
in that way.

VIOLET (*hesitating*). In what way?

L. By giving up your tastes, and sacrificing your feelings, and happiness.

VIOLET. No, no, I don't mean that; but
you know, for other people, one must.

L. For people who don't love you, and
whom you know nothing about? Be it so;
but how does this " giving up " differ from
suicide then?

VIOLET. Why, giving up one's pleasures is
not killing one's self?

L. Giving up wrong pleasure is not; neither is it self-sacrifice, but self-culture. But
giving up right pleasure is. If you surrender
the pleasure of walking, your foot will
wither: you may as well cut it off: if you
surrender the pleasure of seeing, your eyes
will soon be unable to bear the light; you
may as well pluck them out. And to maim
yourself is partly to kill yourself. Do but
go on maiming, and you will soon slay.

VIOLET. But why do you make me think
of that verse then, about the foot and the
eye?

L. You are indeed commanded to cut off
and to pluck out, if foot or eye offend you;
but why *should* they offend you?

VIOLET. I don't know; I never quite understood that.

L. Yet it is a sharp order; one needing to
be well understood if it is to be well obeyed !

When Helen sprained her ankle the other day you saw how strongly it had to be bandaged; that is to say, prevented from all work, to recover it. But the bandage was not "lovely,"

VIOLET. No, indeed.

L. And if her foot had been crushed, or diseased, or snake-bitten, instead of sprained it might have been needful to cut it off. But the amputation would not have been "lovely."

VIOLET. No.

L. Well, if eye and foot are dead already and betray you,—if the light that is in you be darkness, and you feet run into mischief, or are taken in the snare,—it is indeed time to pluck out, and cut off, I think: but, so crippled, you can never be what you might have been otherwise. You enter into life, at best, halt or maimed; and the sacrifice is not beautiful, though necessary.

VIOLET (*after a pause*). But when one sacrifices one's self for others?

L. Why not rather others for you?

VIOLET. Oh! but I couldn't bear that.

L. Then why should they bear it?

DORA (*bursting in indignant*). And Thermopylæ, and Protesilaus, and Marcus Curtius, and Arnold de Winkelried, and Iphigenia and Jephthah's daughter?

L. (*sustaining the indignation unmoved*). And the Samaritan woman's son?

DORA. Which Smaritan woman's?

L. Read 2 Kings VI. 29.

DORA. (*obeys*). How horrid! As if we meant anything like that!

L. You don't seem to me to know in the least what you do mean, children. What practical difference is there between "that," and what you are talking about? The Samaritan children had no voice of their own in the business, it is true; but neither had Iphigenia; the Greek girl was certainly neither boiled, nor eaten; but that only makes a difference in the dramatic effect; not in the principle.

DORA (*biting her lip*). Well, then, tell us what we ought to mean. As if you didn't teach it all to us, and mean it yourself, at this moment, more than we do, if you wouldn't be tiresome!

L. I mean, and always have meant, simply this, Dora;—that the will of God respecting us is that we shall live by each other's happiness, and life; not by each other's misery, or death. I made you read that verse which so shocked you just now, because the relations of parent and child are typical of all beautiful human help. A child may have to die for its parents; but the purpose of Heaven is that it shall rather live for them;—that, not by its sacrifice, but by its strength, its joy, its force of being, it shall be to them renewal of strength; and as the arrow in the hand of the giant. So it is in all other right relations. Men help each

other by their joy, not by their sorrow.
They are not intended to slay themselves
for each other, but to strengthen themselves
for each other.   And among the many apparently beautiful things which turn, through
mistaken use, to utter evil, I am not sure
but that the thoughtlessly meek and self-
sacrificing spirit of good men must be named
as one of the fatalist.   They have so often
been taught that there is a virtue in mere
suffering, as such ; and foolishly to hope that
good may be brought by Heaven out of all
on which Heaven itself has set the stamp of
evil, that we may avoid it,—that they accept
pain and defeat as if these were their appointed portion ; never understanding that
their defeat is not the less to be mourned because it is more fatal to their enemies than
to them.   The one thing that a good man
has to do, and to see done, is justice ; he is
neither to slay himself nor others cause-
lessly : so far from denying himself, since
he is pleased by good, he is to do his utmost
to get his pleasure accomplished.   And I
only wish there were strength, fidelity, and
sense enough, among the good Englishmen
of this day, to render it possible for them to
band together in a vowed brotherhood, to
enforce, by strength of heart and hand, the
doing of human justice among all who came
within their sphere.   And finally, for your
own teaching, observe, although there may
be need for much self-sacrifice and self-

denial in the correction of faults of character, the moment the character is formed, the self-denial ceases. Nothing is really well done, which it costs you pain to do.

VIOLET. But surely, sir, you are always pleased with us when we try to please others, and not ourselves?

L. My dear child, in the daily course and discipline of right life, we must continually and reciprocally submit and surrender in all kind and courteous and affectionate ways : and these submissions and ministries to each other, of which you all know (none better) the practice and the preciousness, are as good for the yielder as the receiver : they strengthen and perfect as much as they soften and refine. But the real sacrifice of all our strength, or life, or happiness to others (though it may be needed, and though all brave creatures hold their lives in their hand, to be given, when such need comes, as frankly as a soldier gives his life in battle), is yet always a mournful and momentary necessity : not the fulfillment of the continuous law of being. Self-sacrifice which is sought after, and triumphed in, is usually foolish ; and calamitous in its issue : and by the sentimental proclamation and pursuit of it, good people have not only made most of their own lives useless, but the whole framework of their religion so hollow, that at this moment, while the English nation, with its lips, pretends to teach every man to " love his neighbor as himself," with its hands and feet it clutches and tramples like a wild beast ; and practically lives, every soul of it that can, on other people's labor. Briefly, the constant duty of every man to his fellows is to ascertain his own powers and special gifts ; and to strengthen them for the help of others. Do you think Titian would have helped the world better by denying himself, and not painting ; or Casella by denying himself, and not singing ! The real virtue is to be ready to sing the moment people ask us ; as he was, even in purgatory. The very word "virtue" means not "conduct" but "strength," vital energy in the heart. Were not you reading about that group of words beginning with V,—vital, virtuous, vigorous, and so on,—in Max Müller, the other day, Sibyl? Can't you tell the others about it?

SIBYL. No, I can't ; will you tell us, please?

L. Not now, it is too late. Come to me some idle time to-morrow, and I'll tell you about it, if all's well. But the gist of it is, children, that you should at least know two Latin words ; recollect that "mors" means death and delaying ; and "vita" means life and growing : and try always, not to mortify yourselves, but to vivify yourselves.

VIOLET. But, then, are we not to mortify our earthly affections? and surely we are to sacrifice ourselves, at least in God's service, if not in man's?

L. Really, Violet, we are getting too serious. I've given you enough ethics for one
talk, I think! Do let us have a little play.
Lily, what were you so busy about, at the
ant-hill in the wood, this morning?

LILY. Oh, it was the ants who were busy,
not I; I was only trying to help them a
little.

L. And they wouldn't be helped, I suppose?

LILY. No, indeed. I can't think why
ants are always so tiresome, when one tries
to help them! They were carrying bits of
stick, as fast as they could, through a piece
of grass; and pulling and pushing, *so* hard;
and tumbling over and over,—it made one
quite pity them; so I took some of the bits
of stick, and carried them forward a little,
where I thought they wanted to put them;
but instead of being pleased, they left them
directly, and ran about looking quite angry
and frightened; and at last ever so many
of them got up my sleeves, and bit me all
over, and I had to come away.

L. I couldn't think what you were about.
I saw your French grammar lying on the
grass behind you, and thought perhaps you
had gone to ask the ants to hear you a
French verb.

ISABEL. Ah! but you didn't, though!

L. Why not, Isabel? I knew, well enough,
Lily couldn't learn that verb by herself.

ISABEL. No; but the ants couldn't help her.

L. Are you sure the ants could not have helped you, Lily?

LILY (*thinking*). I ought to have learned something from them perhaps.

L. But none of them left their sticks to help you through the irregular verb?

LILY. No, indeed. (*Laughing, with some others.*)

L. What are you laughing at, children? I cannot see why the ants should not have left their tasks to help Lily in hers,—since here is Violet thinking she ought to leave *her* tasks, to help God in His. Perhaps, however, she takes Lily's more modest view, and thinks only that "He ought to learn something from her."

(*Tears in* VIOLET'S *eyes.*)

DORA (*scarlet*). It's too bad—it's a shame; —poor Violet!

L. My dear children, there's no reason who one should be so red, and the other so pale, merely because you are made for a moment to feel the absurdity of a phrase which you have been taught to use, in common with half the religious world. There is but one way in which man can ever help God—that is, by letting God help him: and there is no way in which His name is more guiltily taken in vain, than by calling the abandonment of our own work, the performance of His.

God is a kind Father. He sets us all in the places where He wishes us to be employed; and that employment is truly "our Father's business." He chooses work for every creature which will be delightful to them, if they do it simply and humbly. He gives us always strength enough, and sense enough, for what He wants us to do; if we either tire ourselves or puzzle ourselves, it is ourselves, it is our own fault. And we may always be sure, whatever we are doing, that we cannot be pleasing Him, if we are not happy ourselves. Now, away with you, children; and be as happy as you can. And when you cannot, at least don't plume yourselves upon pouting.

LECTURE 7.

HOME VIRTUES.

LECTURE VII.

HOME VIRTUES.

By the fireside, in the Drawing-room. Evening.

DORA. Now, the curtains are drawn, and the fire's bright, and here's your arm-chair—and you're to tell us all about what you promised.

L. All about what?

DORA. All about virtue.

KATHLEEN. Yes, and about the words that begin with V.

L. I heard you singing about a word that begins with V, in the playground, this morning, Miss Katie.

KATHLEEN. Me singing!

MARY. Oh, tell us—tell us.

L. "Vilikens and his—"

KATHLEEN (*stopping his mouth*). Oh! please don't. Where were you?

ISABEL. I'm sure I wish I had known where he was! We lost him among the rhododendrons, and I don't know where he got to; oh, you naughty—naughty—(*climbs on his knee*).

DORA. Now, Isabel, we really want to talk.

133

L. *I* don't.

Dora. Oh, but you must. You promised, you know.

L. Yes, if all was well; but all's ill. I'm tired and cross; and I won't.

Dora. You're not a bit tired, and you're not crosser than two sticks; and we'll make you talk, if you were crosser than six. Come here, Egypt; and get on the other side of him.

(Egypt *takes up a commanding position near the hearth-brush.*)

Dora (*reviewing her forces*). Now, Lily, come and sit on the rug in front.

(Lily *does as she is bid.*)

L. (*seeing he has no chance against the odds.*) Well, well; but I'm really tired. Go and dance a little, first; and let me think.

Dora. No; you mustn't think. You will be wanting to make us think next; that will be tiresome.

L. Well, go and dance first, to get quit of thinking: and then I'll talk as long as you like.

Dora. Oh, but we can't dance to-night. There isn't time; and we want to hear about virtue.

L. Let me see a little of it first. Dancing is the first of girl's virtues.

Egypt. Indeed! And the second?

L. Dressing.

Egypt. Now, you needn't say that! I mended that tear the first thing before breakfast this morning.

L. I cannot otherwise express the ethical principle, Egypt ; whether you have mended your gown or not.

Dora. Now don't be tiresome. We really must hear about virtue, please ; seriously.

L. Well. I'm telling you about it, as fast as I can.

Dora. What the first of girls' virtues is dancing ?

L. More accurately, it is wishing to dance, and not wishing to tease, nor hear about virtue.

Dora (to Egypt). Isn't he cross ?

Egypt. How many balls must we go to in the season, to be perfectly virtuous ?

L. As many as you can without losing your color. But I did not say you should wish to go to balls. I said you should be always wanting to dance.

Egypt. So we do ; but everybody says it is very wrong.

L. Why, Egypt, I thought—

> There was a lady once,
> That would not be a queen,—that would she not
> For all the mud in Egypt.''

You were complaining the other day of having to go out a great deal oftener than you liked.

Egypt. Yes, so I was ; but then, it isn't to dance. There's no room to dance ; it's— (*Pausing to consider what it is for*).

L. It is only to be seen, I suppose. Well, there's no harm in that. Girls ought to like to be seen.

DORA (*her eyes flashing*). Now, you don't mean that; and you're too provoking; and we won't dance again, for a month.

L. It will answer every purpose of revenge, Dora, if you only banish me to the library; and dance by yourselves;. but I don't think Jessie and Lily will agree to that. You like me to see you dancing, don't you, Lily?

LILY. Yes, certainly,—when we do it rightly.

L. And besides, Miss Dora, if young ladies really do not want to be seen, they should take care not let their eyes flash when they dislike what people say: and, more than that, it is all nonsense from beginning to end, about not wanting to be seen. I don't know any more tiresome flower in the borders than your especially "modest" snowdrop; which one always has to stoop down and take all sorts of tiresome trouble with, and nearly break its poor little head off, before you can see it, and then, half of it is not worth seeing. Girls should be like daisies; nice and white, with an edge of red, if you look close; making the ground bright wherever they are; knowing simply and quietly that they do it, and are meant to do it, and that it would be very wrong if they didn't do it. Not want to be seen, indeed!

How long were you in doing up your back hair this afternoon, Jessie?

(JESSIE *not immediately answering*, DORA *comes to her assistance.*)

DORA. Not above three-quarters of an hour, I think, Jess?

JESSIE (*putting her finger up*). Now, Dorothy, *you* needn't talk, you know!

L. I know she needn't, Jessie; I shall ask her about those dark plaits presently. (DORA *looks round to see if there is any way open for retreat.*) But never mind; it was worth the time, whatever it was, and nobody will ever mistake that golden wreath for a chignon : but if you don't want it to be seen you had better wear a cap.

JESSIE. Ah, now, are you really going to do nothing but play? And we all have been thinking, and thinking, all day ; and hoping you would tell us things ; and now—!

L. And now I am telling you things, and true things, and things good for you ; and you won't believe me. You might as well have let me go to sleep at once, as I wanted to. (*Endeavors again to make himself comfortable.*)

ISABEL. Oh, no, no, you sha'n't go to sleep, you naughty !—Kathleen, come here.

L. (*knowing what he has to expect if* KATHLEEN *comes.*) Get away, Isabel, you're too heavy. (*Sitting up.*) What have I been saying?

DORA. I do believe he has been asleep all

the time! You never heard anything like the things you've been saying.

L. Perhaps not. If you have heard them, and anything like them, it is all I want.

EGYPT. Yes, but we don't understand, and you know we don't; and we want to.

L. What did I say first?

DORA. That the first virtue of girls was wanting to go to balls.

L. I said nothing of the kind.

JESSIE. "Always wanting to dance," you said.

L. Yes, and that's true. Their first virtue is to be intensely happy;—so happy that they don't know what to do with themselves for happiness,—and dance, instead of walking. Don't you recollect "Louisa,"

> " No fountain from a rocky cave
> E'er tripped with foot so free;
> She seemed as happy as a wave
> That dances on the sea."

A girl is always like that, when everything's right with her.

VIOLET. But, surely, one must be sad sometimes?

L. Yes, Violet; and dull sometimes, and stupid sometimes, and cross sometimes. What must be, must; but it is always either our own fault, or somebody else's. The last and worst thing that can be said of a nation is, that it has made its young girls sad, and weary.

MAY. But I am sure I have heard a great many good people speak against dancing?

L. Yes, May; but it does not follow they were wise as well as good. I suppose they think Jeremiah liked better to have to write Lamentations for his people, than to have to write that promise for them, which everybody seems to hurry past, tnat they may get on quickly to the verse about Rachel weeping for her children; though the verse they pass is the counter blessing to that one: "Then shall the virgin rejoice in the dance; and both young men and old together; and I will turn their mourning into joy."

(*The children get very serious, but look at each other as if pleased.*)

MARY. They understand now: but, do you know what you said next?

L. Yes; I was not more than half asleep. I said their second virtue was dressing.

MARY. Well! what did you mean by that?

L. What do *you* mean by dressing?

MARY. Wearing fine clothes.

L. Ah! there's the mistake. *I* mean wearing plain ones.

MARY. Yes, I dare say! but that's not what girls understand by dressing, you know.

L. I can't help that. If they understand by dressing, buying dresses, perhaps they also understand by drawing, buying pictures. But when I hear them say they can draw, I understand that they can make a drawing; and when I hear them say they can dress, I

understand that they can make a dress and
—which is quite as difficult—wear one.

DORA. I'm not sure about the making; for
the wearing, we can all wear them—out,
before anybody expects it.

EGYPT (*aside to* L., *piteously*). Indeed I
have mended that torn flounce quite neatly;
look if I haven't!

L. (*aside to* EGYPT). All right; don't be
afraid. (*Aloud to* DORA.) Yes, doubtless;
but you know that is only a slow way of
*un*dressing.

DORA. Then, we are all to learn dress-
making, are we?

L. Yes; and always to dress yourselves
beautifully—not finely, unless on occasion;
but then very finely and beautifully, too.
Also, you are to dress as many other people
as you can; and to teach them how to dress,
if they don't know; and to consider every
ill-dressed woman or child whom you see
anywhere, as a personal disgrace; and to
get at them, somehow, until everybody is
as beautifully dressed as birds.

(*Silence; the children drawing their
breaths hard, as if they had come from
under a shower bath.*)

L. (*seeing objections begin to express themselves in the eyes*). Now you needn't say
you can't; for you can and it's what you
were meant to do, always; and to dress
your houses and your gardens, too; and to
do very little else, I believe, except singing;

and dancing, as we said, of course and—one thing more.

Dora. Our third and last virtue, I suppose?

L. Yes ; on Violet's system of triplicities.

Dora. Well, we are prepared for anything now. What is it ?

L. Cooking.

Dora. Cardinal, indeed ! If only Beatrice were here with her seven handmaids, that she might see what a fine eighth we had found for her !

Mary. And the interpretation ? What does " cooking " mean ?

L. It means the knowledge of Medea, and of Circe, and of Calypso, and of Helen, and of Rebekah, and of the Queen of Sheba. It means the knowledge of all herbs, and fruits, and balms, and spices ; and of all that is heal- ing and sweet in fields and groves, and savory in meats ; it means carefulness, and inventiveness, and watchfulness, and will- ingness, and readiness of appliance ; it means the economy of your great-grandmothers, and the science of modern chemists ; it means much tasting, and no wasting ; it means English thoroughness, and French art, and Arabian hospitality ; it means, in fine, that you are to be perfectly and always "ladies" —" loaf-givers," and, as you are to see, im- peratively, that everybody has something pretty to put on,—so you are to see, yet more imperatively, that everybody has some- thing nice to eat.

(Another pause, and long drawn breath.)

Dora *(slowly recovering herself to* Egypt). We had better have let him go to sleep, I think, after all !

L. You had better let the younger ones go to sleep now : for I haven't half done.

Isabel *(panic-struck).* Oh ! please, please ! just one quarter of an hour.

L. No, Isabel ; I cannot say what I've got to say in a quarter of an hour, and it is too hard for you, besides :—you would be lying awake, and trying to make it out, half the night. That will never do.

Isabel. Oh, please !

L. It would please me exceedingly, mousie : but there are times when we must both be displeased ; more's the pity. Lily may stay for half an hour, if she likes.

Lily. I can't, because Isey never goes to sleep, if she is waiting for me to come.

Isabel. Oh, yes, Lily ; I'll go to sleep to-night. I will, indeed.

Lily. Yes, it's very likely. Isey, with those fine round eyes ! *(To* L.) You'll tell me something of what you've been saying to-morrow, won't you ?

L. No, I won't, Lily. You must choose. It's only in Miss Edgeworth's novels that one can do right, and have one's cake and sugar afterwards, as well (not that I consider the dilemma, to-night, so grave).

(Lily sighing, takes Isabel's hand.)

Yes, Lily dear, it will be better, in the

outcome of it, so, than if you were to hear all the talks that ever were talked, and all the stories that ever were told. Good-night.

(*The door leading to the condemned cells of the Dormitory closes on* LILY, ISABEL, FLORRIE, *and other diminutive and submissive victims.*)

JESSIE (*after a pause*). Why, I thought you were so fond of Miss Edgeworth.

L. So I am ; and so you ought all to be. I can read her over and over again, without ever tiring ; there's no one whose every page is so full, and so delightful ; no one who brings you into the company of pleasanter or wiser people ; no one who tells you more truly how to do right. And it is very nice, in the midst of a wild world, to have the very ideal of poetical justice done always to one's hand :—to have everybody found out, who tells lies ; and everybody decorated with a red ribbon, who doesn't ; and to see the good Laura, who gave away her half sovereign, receiving a grand ovation from an entire dinner party disturbed for the purpose ; and poor, dear, little Rosamond, who chooses purple jars instead of new shoes, left at last without either her shoes or her bottle. But it isn't life : and, in the way children might easily understand it, it isn't morals.

JESSIE. How do you mean we might understand it ?

L. You might think Miss Edgeworth

meant that the right was to be done mainly
because one is always rewarded for doing it.
It is an injustice to her to say that; her
heroines always do right simply for its own
sake, as they should; and her examples of
conduct and motive are wholly admirable.
But her representation of events is false and
misleading. Her good characters never are
brought into the deadly trial of goodness,—
the doing right, and suffering for it, quite
finally. And that is life, as God arranges it.
"Taking up one's cross" does not at all
mean having ovations at dinner parties, and
being put over everybody else's head.

DORA. But what *does* it mean then? That
is just what we couldn't understand, when
you were telling us about not sacrificing
ourselves, yesterday.

L. My dear, it means simply that you are
to go the road which you see to be the
straight one; carrying whatever you find is
given you to carry, as well and stoutly as
you can; without making faces, or calling
people to come and look at you. Above all,
you are neither to load, nor unload, yourself; nor cut your cross to your own liking.
Some people think it would be better for
them to have it large; and many, that they
could carry it much faster if it were small;
and even those who like it largest are usually
very particular about its being ornamental,
and made of the best ebony. But all that
you have really to do is to keep your back as

straight as you can ; and not think about
what is upon it—above all, not to boast of
what is upon it. The real and essential
meaning of "virtue" is in that straightness
of back. Yes; you may laugh, children,
but it is. You know I was to tell you about
the words that began with V. Sibyl, what
does "virtue" mean literally?

SIBYL. Does it mean courage?

L. Yes ; but a particular kind of courage.
It means courage of the nerve ; vital courage. That first syllable of it, if you look in
Max Müller, you will find really means
"nerve," and from it come "vis," and
"vir," and "virgin" (through vireo), and
the connected word "virga"—"a rod ; "—
the green rod, or springing bough of a tree,
being the type of perfect human strength,
both in the use of it in the Mosaic story,
when it becomes a serpent, or strikes
the rock ; or when Aaron's bears its al-
monds ; and in the metaphorical expressions, the "Rod out of the stem of Jesse,"
and the "Man whose name is the Branch,"
and so on. And the essential idea of real
virtue is that of a vital human strength,
which instinctively, constantly, and without
motive, does what is right. You must train
men to this by habit, as you would the
branch of a tree ; and give them instincts
and manners (or morals) of purity, justice,
kindness, and courage. Once rightly
trained, they act as they should irrespect-

10

ively of all motive, of fear, or of reward. It is the blackest sign of putrescence in a national religion, when men speak as if it were the only safeguard of conduct ; and assume that, but for the fear of being burned, or for the hope of being rewarded, everybody would pass their lives in lying, stealing, and murdering. I think quite one of the notablest historical events of this century (perhaps the very notablest), was that council of clergymen, horror-struck at the idea of any diminution in our dread of hell, at which the last of English clergymen whom one would have expected to see in such a function, rose as the devil's advocate ; to tell us how impossible it was we could get on without him.

VIOLET (*after a pause*). But, surely, if people weren't afraid—(*hesitates again*).

L. They should be afraid of doing wrong, and of that only, my dear. Otherwise, if they only don't do wrong for fear of being punished, they *have* done wrong in their hearts already.

VIOLET. Well, but surely, at least one ought to be afraid of displeasing God ; and one's desire to please Him should be one's first motive ?

L. He never would be pleased with us, if it were, my dear. When a father sends his son out into the world—suppose as an apprentice—fancy the boy's coming home at night, and saying, " Father, I could have

robbed the till to-day ; but I didn't, because I thought you wouldn't like it." Do
you think the father would be particularly
pleased ?

(VIOLET *is silent.*)

He would answer, would he not, if he
were wise and good, " My boy, though you
had no father, you must not rob tills " ? And
nothing is ever done so as really to please
our Great Father, unless we would also have
done it, though we had no Father to know
of it.

VIOLET (*after long pause*). But, then,
what continual threatenings, and promises
of reward there are !

L. And how vain both ! with the Jews,
and with all of us. But the fact is, that the
threat and promise are simple statements of
the Divine law, and of its consequences.
The fact is truly told you,—make what use
you may of it : and as collateral warning, or
encouragement, comfort, the knowledge of
future consequences may often be helpful to
us ; but helpful chiefly to the better state
when we can act without reference to them.
And there's no measuring the poisoned influence of that notion of future reward on the
mind of Christian Europe, in the early ages.
Half the monastic system rose out of that,
acting on the occult pride and ambition of
good people (as the other half of it came of
their follies and misfortunes). There is always a considerable quantity of pride, to

begin with, in what is called " giving one's self to God." As if one had ever belonged to anybody else !

DORA. But, surely, great good has come out of the monastic system—our books,—our sciences—all saved by the monks?

L. Saved from what, my dear? From the abyss of misery and ruin which that false Christianity allowed the whole active world to live in. When it had become the principal amusement, and the most admired art of Christian men, to cut one another's throats, and burn one another's towns ; of course the few feeble or reasonable persons left, who desired quiet, safety, and kind fellowship, got into cloisters ; and the gentlest, thoughtfullest, noblest men and women shut themselves up, precisely where they could be of least use. They are very fine things, for us painters, now—the towers and white arches upon the tops of the rocks ; always in places where it takes a day's climbing to get at them ; but the intense tragi-comedy of the thing, when one thinks of it, is unspeakable. All the good people of the world getting themselves hung up out of the way of mischief, like Bailie Nicol Jarvie ;—poor little lambs, as it were, dangling there for the sign of the Golden Fleece ; or like Socrates in his basket in the " Clouds " ! (I must read you that bit of Aristophanes again, by the way.) And believe me, children, I am no warped wit-

ness, as far as regards monasteries ; or if
I am, it is in their favor. I have always
had a strong leaning that way ; and have
pensively shivered with Augustines at St.
Bernard ; and happily made hay with Fran-
ciscans at Fesolé ; and sat silent with Car-
thusians in their little gardens, south of
Florence ; and mourned through many a
day-dream, at Melrose and Bolton. But
the wonder is always to me, not how much,
but how little, the monks have, on the
whole, done, with all that leisure, and all
that good-will ! What nonsense monks
characteristically wrote ;—what little prog-
ress they made in the sciences to which
they devoted themselves as a duty,—medi-
cine especially ; and, last and worst, what
depths of degradation they can sometimes
see one another, and the population round
them, sink into ; without either doubting
their system, or reforming it !

(*Seeing questions rising to lips.*) Hold
your little tongues, children ; it's very late,
and you'll make me forget what I've to say.
Fancy yourselves in pews, for five minutes.
There's one point of possible good in the
conventual system, which is always attrac-
tive to young girls ; and the idea is a very
dangerous one ;—the notion of a merit, or
exalting virtue, consisting in a habit of meditation on the "things above," or things of
the next world. Now it is quite true, that a
person of beautiful mind, dwelling on what-

ever appears to them most desirable and
lovely in a possible future, will not only pass
their time pleasantly, but will even acquire,
at last, a vague and wildly gentle charm of
manner and feature, which will give them
an air of peculiar sanctity in the eyes of
others. Whatever real or apparent good
there may be in this result, I want you to
observe, children, that we have no real authority for the reveries to which it is owing.
We are told nothing distinctly of the heavenly
world; except that it will be free from sorrow, and pure from sin. What is said of
pearl gates, golden floors, and the like, is
accepted as merely figurative by religious
enthusiasts themselves; and whatever they
pass their time in conceiving, whether of the
happiness of risen souls, of their intercourse,
or of the appearance and employment of the
heavenly powers, is entirely the product of
their own imagination; and as completely
and distinctly a work of fiction, or romantic
invention, as any novel of Sir Walter Scott's.
That the romance is founded on religious
theory or doctrine;—that no disagreeable
or wicked persons are admitted into the
story;—and that the inventor fervently hopes
that some portion of it may hereafter come
true, does not in the least alter the real nature
of the effort or enjoyment.

Now, whatever indulgence may be granted
to amiable people for pleasing themselves
in this innocent way, it is beyond question,

that to seclude themselves from the rough
duties of life, merely to write religious ro-
mances, or, as in most cases merely to dream,
them, without taking so much trouble as is
implied in writing, ought not to be received
as an act of heroic virtue. But, observe,
even in admitting thus much, I have as-
sumed that the fancies are just and beautiful,
though fictitious. Now what right have any
of us to assume that our own fancies will
assuredly be either the one or the other?
That they delight us, and appear lovely to
us, is no real proof of its not being wasted
time to form them : and we may surely be
led somewhat to distrust our judgment of
them by observing what ignoble imagina-
tions have sometimes sufficiently, or even
enthusiastically occupied the hearts of others.
The principal source of the spirit of religious
contemplation is the East ; now I have here
in my hand a Byzantine image of Christ,
which, if you will look at it seriously, may,
I think, at once and forever render you cau-
tious in the indulgence of a merely contem-
plative habit of mind. Observe, it is the
fashion to look at such a thing only as a
piece of barbarous art ; that is the smallest
part of its interest. What I want you to see
is the baseness and falseness of a religious
state of enthusiasm in which such a work
could be dwelt upon with pious pleasure.
That a figure, with two small round black
beads for eyes ; a gilded face, deep cut into,

horrible wrinkles ; an open gash for a mouth, and a distorted skeleton for a body, wrapped about, to make it fine, with striped enamel of blue and gold ; that such a figure, I say, should ever have been thought helpful towards the conception of a Redeeming Deity, may make you, I think, very doubtful, even of the Divine approval,—much more of the Divine inspiration,—of religious reverie in general.   You feel, doubtless, that your own idea of Christ would be something very different from this ; but in what does the difference consist ?   Not in any more divine authority in your imagination ; but in the intellectual work of six intervening centuries ; which, simply, by artistic discipline, has refined this crude conception for you, and filled you, partly with an innate sensation, partly with an acquired knowledge, of higher forms,—which render this Byzantine crucifix as horrible to you, as it was pleasing to its maker. More is required to excite your fancy ; but your fancy is of no more authority than his was : and a point of national art-skill is quite conceivable, in which the best we can do now will be as offensive to the religious dreamers of the more highly cultivated time, as this Byzantine crucifix is to you.

MARY. But surely, Angelico will always retain his power over everybody ?

L. Yes, I should think, always ; as the gentle words of a child will : but you would be much surprised, Mary, if you thoroughly took the pains to analyze, and had the perfect means of analyzing, that power of Angelico,—to discover its real sources. Of course it is natural, at first, to attribute it to the pure religious fervor by which he was inspired ; but do you suppose Angelico was really the only monk, in all the Christian world of the middle ages, who labored, in art, with a sincere religious enthusiasm?

MARY. No, certainly not.

L. Anything more frightful, more destructive of all religious faith whatever, than such a supposition, could not be. And yet, what other monk ever produced such work? I have myself examined carefully upwards of two thousand illuminated missals, with especial view to the discovery of any evidence of a similar result upon the art, from the monkish devotion ; and utterly in vain.

MARY. But then, was not Fra Angelico a man of entirely separate and exalted genius?

L. Unquestionably ; and granting him to be that, the peculiar phenomenon in his art is, to me, not its loveliness, but its weakness. The effect of "inspiration," had it been real, on a man of consummate genius, should have been, one would have thought, to make everything that he did faultless and strong, no less than lovely. But of all men, deserving to be called "great," Fra Angelico permits to himself the least pardonable faults, and the most palpable follies. There is evidently within him a sense of grace, and

power of invention, as great as Ghiberti's :—
we are in the habit of attributing those high
qualities to his religious enthusiasm ; but,
if they were produced by that enthusiasm
in him, they ought to be produced by the
same feelings in others ; and we see they
are not. Whereas, comparing him with
contemporary great artists, of equal grace
and invention, one peculiar character remains notable in him—which, logically, we
ought therefore to attribute to the religious
fervor ;—and that distinctive character is,
the contented indulgence of his own weaknesses, and perseverance in his own igno-
rances.

MARY. But that's dreadful ! And what *is*
the source of the peculiar charm which we
all feel in his word ?

L. There are many sources of it, Mary ;
united and seeming like one. You would
never feel that charm but in the work of an
entirely good man ; be sure of that ; but the
goodness is only the recipient and modify-
ing element, not the creative one. Consider
carefully what delights you in any original
picture of Angelico's. You will find, for
one minor thing, an exquisite variety and
brightness of ornamental work. That is not
Angelico's inspiration. It is the final result
of the labor and thought of millions of artists,
of all nations ; from the earliest Egyptian
potters downwards—Greeks, Byzantines,
Hindoos, Arabs, Gauls, and Northmen—all

joining in the toil; and consummating it in Florence, in that century, with such embroidery of robe and inlaying of armor as had never been seen till then ; nor probably, ever will be seen more. Angelico merely takes his share of this inheritance, and applies it in the tenderest way to subjects which are peculiarly acceptant of it. But the inspiration, if it exists anywhere, flashes on the knight's shield quite as radiantly as on the monk's picture. Examining farther into the source of your emotions in the Angelico work, you will find much of the impression of sanctity dependent on a singular repose and grace of gesture, consummating itself in the floating, flying, and above all, in the dancing groups. That is not Angelico's inspiration. It is only a peculiarly tender use of systems of grouping which had been long before developed by Giotto, Memmi, and Orcagna ; and the real root of it all is simply—What do you think, children? The beautiful dancing of the Florentine maidens!

Dora (*indignant again*). Now, I wonder what next! Why not say it all depended on Herodias' daughter, at once?

L. Yes ; it is certainly a great argument against singing that there were once sirens.

Dora. Well, it may be all very fine and philosophical, but shouldn't I just like to read you the end of the second volume of "Modern Painters"!

L. My dear, do you think any teacher
could be worth your listening to, or anybody
else's listening to, who had learned nothing,
and altered his mind in nothing, from seven
and twenty to seven and forty ? But that
second volume is very good for you as far
as it goes. It is a great advance, and a
thoroughly straight and swift one, to be led,
as it is the main business of that second
volume to lead you, from Dutch cattle-pieces,
and ruffian-pieces, to Fra Angelico. And
it is right for you also, as you grow older,
to be strengthened in the general sense and
judgment which may enable you to distin-
guish the weaknesses from the virtues of
what you love, else you might come to love
both alike ; or even the weaknesses without
the virtues. You might end by liking Over-
beck and Cornelius as well as Angelico.
However, I have perhaps been leaning a
little too much to the merely practical side
of things, in to-night's talk ; and you are
always to remember, children, that I do not
deny, though I cannot affirm, the spiritual
advantages resulting, in certain cases, from
enthusiastic religious reverie, and from the
other practices of saints and anchorites.
The evidence respecting them has never yet
been honestly collected, much less dispas-
sionately examined : but assuredly, there is
in that direction a probability, and more
than a probability, of dangerous error, while
there is none whatever in the practice of an

active, cheerful, and benevolent life. The
hope of attaining a higher religious position,
which induces us to encounter, for its exalted
alternative, the risk of unhealthy error, is
often, as I said, founded more on pride than
piety ; and those who, in modest useful-
ness, have accepted what seemed to them
here the lowliest place in the kingdom of
their Father, are not, I believe, the least
likely to receive hereafter the command,
then unmistakable, "Friend, go up higher."

LECTURE 8.
CRYSTAL CAPRICE.

LECTURE VIII.

CRYSTAL CAPRICE.

*Formal Lecture in Schoolroom, after some practical ex-
amination of minerals*

L. We have seen enough, children, though
very little of what might be seen if we had
more time, of mineral structures produced
by visible opposition, or contest among
elements ; structures of which the variety,
however great, need not surprise us : for we
quarrel, ourselves, for many and slight
causes ;—much more, one should think,
may crystals, who can only feel the antag-
onism, not argue about it. But there is a
yet more singular mimicry of our human
ways in the varieties of form which appear
owing to no antagonistic force ; but merely
to the variable humor and caprice of the
crystals themselves : and I have asked you
all to come into the schoolroom to-day,
because, of course, this is a part of the crystal mind which must be peculiarly interesting to a feminine audience. (*Great symptoms of disapproval on the part of said
audience.*) Now you need not pretend that

it will not interest you ; why should it not ?
It is true that we men are never capricious ;
but that only makes us the more dull and
disagreeable. You, who are crystalline in
brightness, as well as in caprice, charm infinitely, by infinitude of change. (*Audible
murmurs of " Worse and worse !" " As if
we could be got over that way !"*. *Etc. The*
LECTURER, *however, observing the expression
of the features to be more complacent, proceeds.*) And the most curious mimicry, if
not of your changes of fashion, at least of
your various modes (in healthy periods) of
national costume, takes place among the
crystals of different countries. With a little
experience, it is quite possible to say at a
glance, in what districts certain crystals
have been found ; and although, if we had
knowledge extended and accurate enough,
we might of course ascertain the laws and
circumstances which have necessarily produced the form peculiar to each locality, this
would be just as true of the fancies of the
human mind. If we could know the exact
circumstances which affect it, we could fore-
tell what now seems to us only caprice of
thought, as well as what now seems to us
only caprice of crystal : nay, so far as our
knowledge reaches, it is on the whole easier
to find some reason why the peasant girls
of Berne should wear their caps in the shape
of butterflies ; and the peasant girls of
Munich theirs in the shape of shells, than to

say why the rock-crystals of Dauphine
should all have their summits of the shape
of lip-pieces of flageolets, while those of St.
Gothard are symmetrical ; or why the fluor
of Chamouni is rose-colored, and in octahedrons, while the fluor of Weardale is green,
and in cubes. Still farther removed is the
hope, at present, of accounting for minor
differences in modes of grouping and construction. Take, for instance, the caprices
of this single mineral, quartz ;—variations
upon a single theme. It has many forms ;
but see what it will make out of this *one*,
the six-sided prism. For shortness' sake,
I shall call the body of the prism its
"column," and the pyramid at the extremi-
ties its "cap." Now, here first you have a
straight column, as long and thin as a stalk
of asparagus, with two little caps at the
ends ; and here you have a short thick
column, as solid as a haystack, with two fat
caps at the ends ; and here you have two
caps fastened together, and no column at
all between them ! Then here is a crystal
with its column fat in the middle, and taper-
ing to a little cap ; and here is one stalked
like a mushroom, with a huge cap put on
the top of a slender column ! Then here is
a column built wholly out of little caps, with
a large smooth cap at the top. And here is
a column built of columns and caps ; the
caps all truncated about half-way to their
points. And in both these last, the little

crystals are set anyhow, and build the large one in a disorderly way ; but here is a crystal made of columns and truncated caps, set in regular terraces all the way up.

MARY. But are not these groups of crystals, rather than one crystal ?

L. What do you mean by a group, and what by one crystal ?

DORA (*audibly aside, to* MARY, *wl o is brought to pause*). You know you are never expected to answer, Mary.

L. I'm sure this is easy enough. What do you mean by a group of people ?

MARY. Three or four together, or a good many together, like the caps in these crystals.

L. But when a great many persons get together they don't take the shape of one person ?

(MARY *still at pause.*)

ISABEL. No, because they can't ; but you know the crystals can ; so why shouldn't they ?

L. Well, they don't ; that is to say, they don't always, nor even often. Look here, Isabel.

ISABEL. What a nasty ugly thing !

L. I'm glad you think it so ugly. Yet it is made of beautiful crystals ; they are a little gray and cold in color, but most of them are clear.

ISABEL. But they're in such horrid, horrid disorder !

L. Yes; all disorder is horrid, when it is
among things that are naturally orderly.
Some little girls' rooms are naturally *dis*orderly, I suppose; or I don't know how they
could live in them, if they cry out so when
they only see quartz crystals in confusion.

ISABEL. Oh ! but how come they to be like
that ?

L. You may well ask. And yet you will
always hear people talking as if they thought
order more wonderful than disorder ! It
is wonderful—as we have seen ; but to me,
as to you, child, the supremely wonderful
thing is that nature should ever be ruinous,
or wasteful, or deathful ! I look at this wild
piece of crystallization with endless astonishment.

MARY. Where does it come from ?

L. The Tête Noire of Chamounix. What
makes it more strange is that it should be in
a vain of fine quartz. If it were in a moldering rock, it would be natural enough ; but
in the midst of so fine substance, here are
the crystals tossed in a heap ; some large,
myriads small (almost as small as dust),
tumbling over each other like a terrified
crowd, and glued together by the sides, and
edges, and backs, and heads ; some warped,
and some pushed out and in, and all spoiled,
and each spoiling the rest.

MARY. And how flat they all are !

L. Yes ; that's the fashion at the **Tête
Noire.**

MARY. But surely this is ruin, not caprice !

L. I believe it is in great part misfortune ;
and we will examine these crystal troubles
in next lecture. But if you want to see the
gracefullest and happiest caprices of which
dust is capable, you must go to the Hartz;
not that I ever mean to go there myself, for
I want to retain the romantic feeling about
the name ; and I have done myself some
harm already by seeing the monotonous and
heavy form of the Brocken from the suburbs
of Brunswick. But whether the mountains
be picturesque or not, the tricks which the
goblins (as I am told) teach the crystals in
them, are incomparably pretty. They work
chiefly on the mind of a docile, bluish-
colored carbonate of lime; which comes
out of a gray limestone. The goblins take
the greatest possible care of its education,
and see that nothing happens to it to hurt
its temper ; and when it may be supposed
to have arrived at the crisis which is to a
well brought up mineral, what presentation
at court is to a young lady—after which it
is expected to set fashions—there's no end
to its pretty ways of behaving. First it will
make itself into pointed darts as fine as hoar-
frost ; here, it is changed into a white fur as
fine as silk ; here into little crowns and cir-
clets, as bright as silver, as if for the gnome
princesses to wear ; here it is in beautiful
little plates, for them to eat off ; presently it

is in towers which they might be imprisoned
in ; presently in caves and cells, where they
may make nun-gnomes of themselves, and
no gnome ever hear of them more ; here is
some of it in sheaves, like corn ; here, some
in drifts, like snow ; here, some in rays, like
stars : and, though these are, all of them,
necessarily, shapes that the mineral takes in
other places, they are all taken here with
such a grace that you recognize the high
caste and breeding of the crystals wherever
you meet them, and know at once they are
Hartz-born.

Of course, such fine things as these are
only done by crystals which are perfectly
good, and good-humored ; and of course,
also, there are ill-humored crystals who tor-
ment each other, and annoy quieter crystals,
yet without coming to anything like serious
war. Here (for once) is some ill-disposed
quartz, tormenting a peaceable octahedron
of fluor, in mere caprice. I looked at it the
other night so long, and so wonderingly,
just before putting my candle out, that I fell
into another strange dream. But you don't
care about dreams.

DORA. No ; we didn't, yesterday ; but you
know we are made up of caprice ; so we do,
to-day : and you must tell it us directly.

L. Well, you see, Neith and her work
were still much in my mind ; and then, I
had been looking over these Hartz things for
you, and thinking of the sort of grotesque

sympathy there seemed to be in them with
the beautiful fringe and pinnacle work of
Northern architecture.　So, when I fell
asleep, I thought I saw Neith and St. Barbara talking together.

DORA. But what had St. Barbara to do with
it ? *

L. My dear, I am quite sure St. Barbara
is the patroness of good architects ; not St.
Thomas, whatever the old builders thought.
It might be very fine, according to the
monks' notions, in St. Thomas, to give all
his employer's money away to the poor :
but breaches of contract are bad foundations ; and I believe, it was not he but St.
Barbara, who overlooked the work in all the
buildings you and I care about.　However
that may be, it was certainly she whom I
saw in my dream with Neith.　Neith was
sitting weaving, and I thought she looked
sad, and drew her shuttle slowly ; and St.
Barbara was standing at her side, in a stiff
little gown, all ins and outs, and angles ;
but so bright with embroidery that it dazzled
me whenever she moved ; the train of it was
just like a heap of broken jewels, it was so
stiff, and full of corners, and so many-colored,
and bright.　Her hair fell over her shoulders
in long, delicate waves, from under a little
three-pinnacled crown, like a tower.　She
was asking Neith about the laws of architect-

* Note v.

ure in Egypt and Greece; and when Neith
told her the measures of the pyramids, St.
Barbara said she thought they would have
been better three-cornered : and when Neith
told her the measures of the Parthenon, St.
Barbara said she thought it ought to have
had two transepts. But she was pleased
when Neith told her of the temple of the
dew, and of the Caryan maidens bearing its
frieze : and then she thought that perhaps
Neith would like to hear what sort of temples
she was building herself, in the French val-
leys, and on the crags of the Rhine. So she
began gossiping, just as one of you might
to an old lady : and certainly she talked in
the sweetest way in the world to Neith ; and
explained to her all about crockets and pinnacles : and Neith sat, looking very grave ;
and always graver as St. Barbara went on ;
till at last, I'm sorry to say, St. Barbara lost
her temper a little.

MAY (*very grave herself*). "St. Barbara ? "

L. Yes, May. Why shouldn't she ? It
was very tiresome of Neith to sit looking
like that.

MAY. But, then, St. Barbara was a saint !

L. What's that, May ?

MAY. A saint ! A saint is—I am sure you
know !

L. If I did, it would not make me sure
that you knew too, May : but I don't.

VIOLET (*expressing the incredulity of the
audience*). Oh,—sir !

L. That is to say, I know that people are
called saints who are supposed to be better
than others : but I don't know how much
better they must be, in order to be saints ; nor
how nearly anybody may be a saint, and yet
not be quite one ; nor whether everybody
who is called a saint was one; nor whether
everybody who isn't called a saint, isn't one.

　*(General silence ; the audience feeling
　themselves on the verge of the Infinities,
　and a little shocked, and much puz-
　zled by so many questions at once.)*

L. Besides, did you never hear that verse
about being " called to be saints "?

MAY (*repeats Rom.* i. 7).

L. Quite right, May. Well, then, who
are called to be that? People in Rome
only?

MAY. Everybody, I suppose, whom God
loves.

L. What! little girls as well as other
people?

MAY. All grown-up people, I mean.

L. Why not little girls? Are they wickeder
when they are little?

MAY. Oh, I hope not.

L. Why not little girls, then?

　(*Pause*).

LILY. Because, you know, we can't be
worth anything if we're ever so good ;—I
mean, if we try to be ever so good ; and we
can't do difficult things—like saints.

L. I am afraid, my dear, that old people

are not more able or willing for their difficulties than you children are for yours. All
I can say is, that if ever I see any of you,
when you are seven or eight and twenty,
knitting your brows over any work you
want to do or to understand, as I saw you,
Lily, knitting your brows over your slate
this morning, I should think you very noble
women. But—to come back to my dream
—St. Barbara *did* lose her temper a little;
and I was not surprised. For you can't think
how provoking Neith looked, sitting there
just like a statue of sandstone; only going
on weaving, like a machine; and never
quickening the cast of her shuttle; while St.
Barbara was telling her so eagerly all about
the most beautiful things, and chattering
away, as fast as bells ring on Christmas
Eve, till she saw that Neith didn't care; and
then St. Barbara got as red as a rose, and
stopped, just in time;—or I think she would
really have said something naughty.

ISABEL. Oh, please, but didn't Neith say
anything then?

L. Yes. She said, quite quietly, "It may
be very pretty, my love; but it is all nonsense."

ISABEL. Oh dear, oh dear; and then?

L. Well; then I was a little angry myself,
and hoped St. Barbara would be quite angry;
but she wasn't. She bit her lips first; and
then gave a great sigh—such a wild, sweet
sigh—and then she knelt down and hid her

face on Neith's knees. Then Neith smiled a little, and was moved.

ISABEL. Oh, I am so glad !

L. And she touched St. Barbara's forehead with a flower of white lotus ; and St. Barbara sobbed once or twice, and then said : "If you only could see how beautiful it is, and how much it makes people feel what is good and lovely ; and if you could only hear the children singing in the Lady chapels ! " And Neith smiled,—but still sadly,—and said, " How do you know what I have seen, or heard, my love? Do you think all those vaults and towers of yours have been built without me? There was not a pillar in your Giotto's Santa Maria del Fiore which I did not set true by my spearshaft as it rose. But this pinnacle and flame work which has set your little heart on fire is all vanity ; and you will soon see what it will come to, and none will grieve for it more than I. And then every one will disbelieve your pretty symbols and types. Men must be spoken simply to, my dear, if you would guide them kindly, and long." But St. Barbara answered, that, "Indeed she thought every one liked her work," and that "the people of different towns were as eager about their cathedral towers as about their privileges or their markets ; " and then she asked Neith to come and build something with her, wall against tower ; and "see whether the people will be as much pleased

with your building as with mine." But Neith
answered, "I will not contend with you,
my dear. I strive not with those who love
me, and for those who hate me, it is not
well to strive with me, as weaver Arachne
knows. And remember, child, that nothing
is ever done beautifully, which is done in
rivalship ; nor nobly, which is done in pride."

Then St. Barbara hung her head quite
down, and said she was very sorry she had
been so foolish; and kissed Neith; and
stood thinking a minute : and then her eyes
got bright again, and she said, she would
go directly and build a chapel with five
windows in it ; four for the four cardinal
virtues, and one for humility, in the middle,
bigger than the rest. And Neith very nearly
laughed quite out, I thought ; certainly her
beautiful lips lost all their sternness for an
instant ; then she said, "Well, love, build
it, but do not put so many colors into your
windows as you usually do ; else no one
will be able to see to read, inside : and
when it is built, let a poor village priest con-
secrate it, and not an archbishop." St.
Barbara started a little, I thought, and
turned as if to say something ; but changed
her mind, and gathered up her train, and
went out. And Neith bent herself again to
her loom, in which she was weaving a web
of strange dark colors, I thought ; but perhaps it was only after the glittering of St.
Barbara's embroidered train ; and I tried to

make out the figures in Neith's web, and
confused myself among them, as one always does in dreams ; and then the dream
changed altogether, and I found myself, all
at once, among a crowd of little Gothic and
Egyptian spirits, who were quarreling ; at
least the Gothic ones were trying to quarrel ;
for the Egyptian ones only sat with their
hands on their knees, and their aprons sticking
out very stiffly ; and stared. And after awhile
I began to understand what the matter was.
It seemed that some of the troublesome
building imps, who meddle and make continually, even in the best Gothic work, had
been listening to St. Barbara's talk with
Neith ; and had made up their minds that
Neith had no workpeople who could build
against them. They were but dull imps, as
you may fancy, by their thinking that ; and
never had done much, except disturbing the
great Gothic building angels at their work,
and playing tricks to each other ; indeed, of
late they had been living years and years,
like bats, up under the cornices of Stras-
bourg and Cologne cathedrals, with nothing
to do but to make mouths at the people
below. However, they thought they knew
everything about tower building ; and those
who had heard what Neith said, told the
rest ; and they all flew down directly, chattering in German, like jackdaws, to show
Neith's people what they could do. And
they had found some of Neith's old work-

people somewhere near Sais, sitting in the sun, with their hands on their knees ; and abused them heartily : and Neith's people did not mind at first, but, after awhile, they seemed to get tired of the noise ; and one or two rose up slowly, and laid hold of their measuring rods, and said, "If St. Barbara's people liked to build with them, tower against pyramid, they would show them how to lay stones." Then the Gothic little spirits threw a great many double somersaults for joy ; and put the tips of their tongues out slyly to each other, on one side ; and I heard the Egyptians say, "they must be some new kind of frog—they didn't think there was much building in *them*." However, the stiff old workers took their rods, as I said, and measured out a square space of sand ; but as soon as the German spirits saw that, they declared they wanted exactly that bit of ground to build on themselves. Then the Egyptian builders offered to go farther off, and the German ones said, "Ja wohl." But as soon as the Egyptians had measured out another square, the little Germans said they must have some of that too. Then Neith's people laughed ; and said, "they might take as much as they liked, but they would not move the plan of their pyramid again." Then the little Germans took three pieces, and began to build three spires directly ; one large, and two little, And when the Egyptians saw they

had fairly begun, they laid their foundation all round, of large square stones : and
began to build, so steadily that they had
like to have swallowed up the three little
German spires.   So when the Gothic spirits
saw that, they built their spires leaning, like
the tower of Pisa, that they might stick out
at the side of the pyramid.   And Neith's
people stared at them ; and thought it very
clever, but very wrong ; and on they went,
in their own way, and said nothing.   Then
the little Gothic spirits were terribly pro-
voked because they could not spoil the
shape of the pyramid ; and they sat down
all along the ledges of it to make faces ;
but that did no good.   Then they ran to
the corners, and put their elbows on their
knees, and stuck themselves out as far as
they could, and made more faces ; but
that did no good, neither.   Then they
looked up to the sky, and opened their
mouths wide, and gobbled, and said it was
too hot for work, and wondered when it
would rain ; but that did no good, neither.
And all the while the Egyptian spirits were
laying step above step, patiently.   But when
the Gothic ones looked, and saw how high
they had got, they said, "Ach, Himmel ! "
and flew down in a great black cluster to
the bottom ; and swept out a level spot in
the sand with their wings, in no time, and
began building a tower straight up, as fast
as they could.   And the Egyptians stood

still again to stare at them ; for tne Gothic
spirits had got quite into a passion, and
were really working very wonderfully.
They cut the sandstone into strips as fine as
reeds ; and put one reed on the top of
another, so that you could not see where
they fitted : and they twisted them in and
out like basket work, and knotted them into
likenesses of ugly faces, and of strange
beasts biting each other ; and up they went,
and up still, and they made spiral staircases
at the corners, for the loaded workers to
come up by (for I saw they were but weak
imps, and could not fly with stones on their
backs), and then they made traceried gal-
leries for them to run round by ; and so up
again ; with finer and finer work, till the
Egyptians wondered whether they meant
the thing for a tower or a pillar : and I
heard them saying to one another, "It was
nearly as pretty as lotos stalks ; and if it
were not for the ugly faces there would be a
fine temple, if they were going to build it
all with pillars as big as that !" But in a
minute afterwards,—just as the Gothic spirits
had carried their work as high as the upper
course, but three or four, of the pyramid—
the Egyptians called out to them to "mind
what they were about, for the sand was
running away from under one of their tower
corners." But it was too late to mind what
they were about ; for, in another instant, the
whole tower sloped aside ; and the Gothic

12

imps rose out of it like a flight of puffins, in a single cloud; but screaming worse than any puffins you ever heard : and down came the tower, all in a piece, like a falling poplar, with its head right on the flank of the pyramid; against which it snapped short off.   And of course that waked me!

MARY. What a shame of you to have such a dream, after all you have told us about Gothic architecture!

L. If you have understood anything I ever told you about it, you know that no architecture was ever corrupted more miserably; or abolished more justly by the accomplishment of its own follies. Besides, even in its days of power, it was subject to catastrophes of this kind.   I have stood too often, mourning, by the grand fragment of the apse of Beauvais, not to have that fact well burnt into me.   Still, you must have seen, surely, that these imps were of the Flamboyant school; or, at least, of the German schools correspondent with it in extravagance.

MARY. But, then, where is the crystal about which you dreamed all this?

L. Here ; but I suppose little Pthah has touched it again, for it is very small.   But, you see, here is the pyramid, built of great square stones of fluor spar, straight up ; and here are the three little pinnacles of mischievous quartz, which have set themselves, at the same time, on the same foun-

dation; only they lean like the tower of
Pisa, and come out obliquely at the side;
and here is one great spire of quartz which
seems as if it had been meant to stand
straight up, a little way off; and then had
fallen down against the pyramid base,
breaking its pinnacle away. In reality, it
has crystallized horizontally, and terminated
imperfectly: but then, by what caprice
does one crystal form horizontally, when all
the rest stand upright? But this is nothing
to the phantasies of fluor, and quartz, and
some other such companions, when they
get leave to do anything they like. I could
show you fifty specimens, about every one
of which you might fancy a new fairy tale.
Not that, in truth, any crystals get leave to
do quite what they like; and many of them
are sadly tried, and have little time for caprices—poor things!

MARY. I thought they always looked as if
they were either in play or in mischief?
What trials have they?

L. Trials much like our own. Sickness,
and starvation; fevers, and agues, and
palsy; oppression; and old age, and the
necessity of passing away in their time, like
all else. If there's any pity in you, you
must come to-morrow, and take some part
in these crystal griefs.

DORA. I am sure we shall cry till our eyes
are red.

L. Ah, you may laugh, Dora: but I've

been made grave, not once, nor twice, to
see that even crystals "cannot choose but
be old" at last. It may be but a shallow
proverb of the Justice's; but is a shrewdly
wise one.

DORA (*pensive for once*). I suppose it *is*
very dreadful to be old ! But then (*bright-
ening again*), what should we do without
our dear old friends, and our nice old lectures ?

L. If all nice old lecturers were minded
as little as one I know of—

DORA. And if they all meant as little what
they say, would they not deserve it ? But
we'll come,—we'll come, and cry.

LECTURE 9.

CRYSTAL SORROWS.

LECTURE IX.

Working Lecture in Schoolroom.

L. We have been hitherto talking, children, as if crystals might live, and play, and quarrel, and behave ill or well, according to their characters without interruption from anything else. But so far from this being so, nearly all crystals, whatever their characters, have to live a hard life of it, and meet with many misfortunes. It we could see far enough, we should find, indeed, that, at the root, all their vices were misfortunes; but to-day I want you to see what sort of troubles the best crystals have to go through, occasionally, by no fault of their own.

This black thing, which is one of the prettiest of the very few pretty black things in the world, is called "Tourmaline." It may be transparent, and green, or red, as well as black; and then no stone can be prettier (only, all the light that gets into it, I believe, comes out a good deal the worse; and is not itself again for a long while). But this is the commonest state of it,—opaque, and as black as jet.

183

MARY. What does "Tourmaline" mean?

L. They say it is Ceylanese, and I don't know Ceylanese; but we may always be thankful for a graceful word, whatever it means.

MARY. And what is it made of?

L. A little of everything; there's always flint, and clay, and magnesia in it ; and the black is iron, according to its fancy; and there's boracic acid, if you know what that is; and if you don't, I cannot tell you to-day ; and it doesn't signify : and there's pot-ash, and soda ; and, on the whole, the chemistry of it is more like a mediæval doc-tor's prescription, than the making of a re-spectable mineral : but it may, perhaps, be owing to the strange complexity of its make, that it has a notable habit which makes it, to me, one of the most interesting of minerals. You see these two crystals are broken right across, in many places, just as if they had been shafts of black marble fallen from a ruinous temple ; and here they lie, imbedded in white quartz, fragment succeeding frag-ment, keeping the line of the original crystal, while the quartz fills up the intervening spaces.   Now Tourmaline has a trick of do-ing this, more than any other mineral I know ; here is another bit which I picked up on the glacier of Macugnaga : it is broken, like a pillar built of very flat broad stones, into about thirty joints, and all these are heaved and warped away from each other sideways, almost into a line of steps; and then all is filled up with quartz paste. And here, lastly, is a green Indian piece, in which the pillar is first disjointed, and then wrung round into the shape of an S.

MARY. How *can* this have been done?

L. There are a thousand ways in which it may have been done; the difficulty is not to account for the doing of it; but for the showing of it in some crystals, and not in others. You never by any chance get a quartz crystal broken or twisted in this way. If it break or twist at all, which it does sometimes, like the spire of Dijon, it is by its own will or fault; it never seems to have been passively crushed. But, for the forces which cause this passive ruin of the tourmaline,—here is a stone which will show you multitudes of them in operation at once. It is known as "brecciated agate," beautiful, as you see; and highly valued as a pebble : yet, so far as I can read or hear, no one has ever looked at it with the least attention. At the first glance, you see it is made of very fine red striped agates, which have been broken into small pieces, and fastened together again by paste, also of agate. There would be nothing wonderful in this, if this were all. It is well-known that by the movements of strata, portions of rock are often shattered to pieces :—well known also that agate is a deposit of flint by water under certain conditions of heat and pressure : there is, therefore, nothing wonderful in an agate's being broken ; and nothing wonderful in its being mended with the solution out of which it was itself originally congealed. And with this explanation most people looking at a brecciated agate, or brecciated anything, seem to be satisfied. I was so myself, for twenty years; but, lately happening to stay for some time at the Swiss Baden, where the beach of the Limmat is almost wholly composed of brecciated limestones, I began to examine them thoughtfully ; and perceived, in the end, that they were, one and all, knots of as rich mystery as any poor little human brain was ever lost in. That piece of agate in your hand, Mary, will show you many of the common phenomena of breccias ; but you need not knit your brows over it in that way ; depend upon it, neither you nor I shall ever know anything about the way it was made, as long as we live.

DORA. That does not seem much to depend upon.

L. Pardon me, puss. When once we gain some real notion of the extent and unconquerableness of our ignorance, it is a very broad and restful thing to depend upon : you can throw yourself upon it at ease, as on a cloud to feast with the gods. You do not thenceforward trouble yourself,—nor any one else,—with theories, or the contradiction of theories ; you neither get head-

ache nor heart-burning ; and you never more
waste your poor little store of strength or
allowance of time.

However, there are certain facts, about
this gate-making, which I can tell you;
and then you may look at it in ɂ pleasant
wonder as long as you like ; pleasant wonder is no loss of time.

First, then, it is not broken freely by a
blow ; it is slowly wrung, or ground, to
pieces. You can only with extreme dim-
ness conceive the force exerted on mountains in transitional states of movement.
You have all read a little geology ; and you
know how coolly geologists talk of mountains being raised or depressed. They talk
coolly of it, because they are accustomed to
the fact ; but the very universality of the
fact prevents us from ever conceiving distinctly the conditions of force involved. You
know I was living last year in Savoy ; my
house was on the back of a sloping mountain, which rose gradually for two miles
behind it ; and then fell at once in a great
precipice toward Geneva, going down three
thousand feet in four or five cliffs, or steps.
Now that whole group of cliffs had simply
been torn away by sheer strength from the
rocks below, as if the whole mass had been
as soft as biscuit. Put four or five captains'
biscuits on the floor, on the top of one
another ; and try to break them all in half,
not by bending, but by holding one half

down, and tearing the other halves straight
up ;—of course you will not be able to do it,
but you will feel and comprehend the sort
of force needed. Then, fancy each captains'
biscuit a bed of rock, six or seven hundred
feet thick ; and the whole mass torn straight
through ; and one half heaved up three
thousand feet, grinding against the other as
it rose,—and you will have some idea of the
making of the Mont Salève.

MAY. But it must crush the rocks all to
dust.

L. No; for there is no room for dust.
The pressure is too great; probably the heat
developed also so great that the rock is made
partly ductile; but the worst of it is, that
we never can see these parts of mountains
in the state they were left in at the time of
their elevation ; for it is precisely in these
rents and dislocations that the crystalline
power principally exerts itself. It is essentially a styptic power, and wherever the earth
is torn, it heals and binds ; nay, the torture
and grieving of the earth seem necessary to
bring out its full energy ; for you only find
the crystalline living powerfully in action,
where the rents and faults are deep and
many.

DORA. If you please, sir,—would you tell
us—what are " faults " ?

L. You never heard of such things ?

DORA. Never in all our lives.

L. When a vein of rock, which is going on

smoothly, is interrupted by another troublesome little vein, which stops it, and puts it
out so that it has to begin again in another
place—that is called a fault. *I* always think
it ought to be called the fault of the vein
that interrupts it ; but the miners always call
it the fault of the vein that is interrupted.

Dora. So it is, if it does not begin again
where it left off.

L. Well, that is certainly the gist of the
business : but, whatever good-natured old
lecturers may do, the rocks have a bad habit,
when they are once interrupted, of never
asking "Where was I ?"

Dora. When the two halves of the dining
table came separate, yesterday, was that a
"fault"?

L. Yes ; but not the table's. However,
it is not a bad illustration, Dora. When
beds of rock are only interrupted by a fissure,
but remain at the same level, like the two
halves of the table, it is not called a fault,
but only a fissure ; but if one half of the
table be either tilted higher than the other,
or pushed to the side, so that the two parts
will not fit, it is a fault. You had better
read the chapter on faults in Jukes's Geology ;
then you will know all about it. And this
rent that I am telling you of in the Saléve,
is one only of myriads, to which are owing
the forms of the Alps, as, I believe, of all
great mountain chains. Wherever you see
a precipice on any scale of real magnifi-

cence, you will nearly always find it owing to some dislocation of this kind ; but the point of chief wonder to me is, the delicacy of the touch by which these gigantic rents have been apparently accomplished.   Note, however, that we have no clear evidence, hitherto, of the time taken to produce any of them.   We know that a change of temperature alters the position and the angles of the atoms of crystals, and also the entire bulk of rocks.   We know that in all volcanic, and the greater part of all subterranean, action, temperatures are continually changing, and therefore masses of rock must be expanding or contracting, with infinite slowness, but with infinite force.   This pressure must result in mechanical strain somewhere, both in their own substance, and in that of the rocks surrounding them ; and we can form no conception of the result of irresistible pressure, applied so as to rend and raise, with imperceptible slowness of gradation, masses thousands of feet in thickness. We want some experiments tried on masses of iron and stone ; and we can't get them tried, because Christian creatures never will seriously and sufficiently spend money, except to find out the shortest way of killing each other.   But, besides this slow kind of pressure, there is evidence of more or less sudden violence, on the same terrific scale ; and, through it all, the wonder, as I said, is always to me the delicacy of touch.   I cut

a block of the Saléve limestone from the edge
of one of the principal faults which have
formed the precipice; it is a lovely compact
limestone, and the fault itself is filled up with
a red breccia, formed of the crushed fragments of the torn rock, cemented by a rich
red crystalline paste. I have had the piece
I cut from it smoothed, and polished across
the junction; here it is; and you may now
pass your soft little fingers over the surface,
without so much as feeling the place where
a rock which all the hills of England might
have been sunk in the body of, and not a
summit seen, was torn asunder through that
whole thickness, as a thin dress is torn when
you tread upon it.

*(The audience examine the stone, and
touch it timidly, but the matter remains
inconceivable to them.)*

MARY *(struck by the beauty of the stone).*
But this is almost marble?

L. It is quite marble. And another singular point in the business, to my mind, is
that these stones, which men have been cutting into slabs, for thousands of years, to
ornament their principal buildings with,—
and which, under the general name of " marble," have been the delight of the eyes, and
the wealth of architecture, among all civilized nations,—are precisely those on which
the signs and brands of these earth agonies
have been chiefly struck; and there is not a
purple vein nor flaming zone in them, which

is not the record of their ancient torture.
What a boundless capacity for sleep, and for
serene stupidity, there is in the human mind!
Fancy reflective beings, who cut and polish
stones for three thousand years, for the sake
of the pretty stains upon them ; and edu-
cate themselves to an art at last (such as it
is), of imitating these veins by dexterous
painting ; and never a curious soul of them,
all that while, asks, "What painted the
rocks ? "

(*The audience look dejected, and ashamed
of themselves.*)

The fact is, we are all, and always, asleep,
through our lives ; and it is only by pinch-
ing ourselves very hard that we ever come to
see, or understand, anything.   At least, it is
not always we who pinch ourselves ; sometimes other people pinch us ; which I suppose is very good of them,—or other things,
which I suppose is very proper of them.
But it is a sad life ; made up chiefly of naps
and pinches.

(*Some of the audience, on this, appearing
to think that the others require pinch-
ing, the* LECTURER *changes the subject.*)

Now, however, for once, look at a piece
of marble carefully, and think about it.
You see this is one side of the fault ; the
other side is down or up, nobody knows
where : but, on this side, you can trace the
evidence of the dragging and tearing action.
All along the edge of this marble, the ends

of the fibers of the rock are torn, here an inch,
and there half an inch, away from each
other ; and you see the exact places where
they fitted, before they were torn separate :
and you see the rents are now all filled up
with the sanguine paste, full of the broken
pieces of the rock ; the paste itself seems to
have been half melted, and partly to have
also melted the edge of the fragments it contains, and then to have crystallized with
them, and round them. And the brecciated
agate I first showed you contains exactly the
same phenomena ; a zoned crystallization
going on amidst the cemented fragments,
partly altering the structure of those fragments themselves, and subject to continual
change, either in the intensity of its own
power, or in the nature of the materials sub-
mitted to it ;—so that, at one time, gravity
acts upon them, and disposes them in hori-
zontal layers, or causes them to droop in
stalactites ; and at another, gravity is entirely defied, and the substances in solution
are crystallized in bands of equal thickness
on every side of the cell. It would require a
course of lectures longer than these (I have
a great mind—you have behaved so saucily
—to stay and give them) to describe to you
the phenomena of this kind, in agates and
chalcedonies only ;—nay, there is a single
sarcophagus in the British Museum, covered
with grand sculpture of the 18th dynasty,
which contains in magnificent breccia

13

(agates and jaspers imbedded in porphyry),
out of which it is hewn, material for the
thought of years ; and recorded of the earth-
sorrow of ages in comparison with the dura-
tion of which, the Egyptian letters tell us
but the history of the evening and morning
of a day.

Agates, I think, of all stones, confess
most of their past history ; but all crystallization goes on under, and partly records circumstances of this kind—circumstances of
infinite variety, but always involving difficulty, interruption, and change of condition
at different times. Observe, first, you have
the whole mass of the rock in motion, either
contracting itself, and so gradually widen-
ing the cracks ; or being compressed, and
thereby closing them, and crushing their
edges ;—and, if one part of its substance
be softer, at the given temperature, than
another, probably squeezing that softer
substance out into the veins. Then the
veins themselves, when the rock leaves
them open by its contraction, act with
various power of suction upon its substance ;—by capillary attraction when they
are fine,—by that of pure vacuity when
they are larger, or by changes in the con-
stitution and condensation of the mixed
gases with which they have been originally
filled. Those gases themselves may be supplied in all variation of volume and power
from below ; or, slowly, by the decomposi-

tion of the rocks themselves ; and, at changing temperatures, must exert relatively
changing forces of decomposition and com-
bination on the walls of the veins they fill ;
while water, at every degree of heat and
pressure (from beds of everlasting ice, alternate with cliffs of native rock, to volumes of
red hot, or white hot steam), congeals, and
drips, and throbs, and thrills, from crag to
crag ; and breathes from pulse to pulse of
foaming or fiery arteries, whose beating is felt
through chains of the great islands of the Indian seas, as your own pulses lift your brace-
lets, and makes whole kingdoms of the world
quiver in deadly earthquake, as if they were
light as aspen leaves. And, remember, the
poor little crystals have to live their lives,
and mind their own affairs, in the midst of
all this, as best they may. They are wonderfully like human creatures,—forget all
that is going on if they don't see it, however dreadful ; and never think what is to
happen to-morrow. They are spiteful or
loving, and indolent or painstaking, and
orderly or licentious, with no thought whatever of the lava or the flood which may
break over them any day ; and evaporate
them into air-bubbles, or wash them into a
solution of salts. And you may look at
them, once understanding the surrounding
conditions of their fate, with an endless interest. You will see crowds of unfortunate
little crystals, who have been forced to con-

stitute themselves in a hurry, their dissolving element being fiercely scorched away; you will see them doing their best, bright and numberless, but tiny. Then you will find indulged crystals, who have had centuries to form themselves in, and have changed their mind and ways continually; and have been tired, and taken heart again; and have been sick, and got well again; and thought they would try a different diet, and then thought better of it; and made but a poor use of their advantages, after all. And others you will see, who have begun life as wicked crystals; and then have been impressed by alarming circumstances, and have become converted crystals, and behaved amazingly for a little while, and fallen away again, and ended, but discreditably, perhaps even in decomposition; so that one doesn't know what will become of them. And sometimes you will see deceitful crystals, that look as soft as velvet, and are deadly to all near them; and sometimes you will see deceitful crystals, that seem flint-edged, like our little quartz-crystal of a housekeeper here (hush! Dora), and are endlessly gentle and true wherever gentleness and truth are needed. And sometimes you will see little child-crystals put to school like school-girls, and made to stand in rows; and taken the greatest care of, and taught how to hold themselves up, and behave: and sometimes you will see unhappy little child-crystals left to lie about in the dirt, and pick.

up their living, and learn manners where they
can. And sometimes you will see fat crystals eating up thin ones, like great capitalists
and little laborers ; and politico-economic
crystals teaching the stupid ones how to eat
each other, and cheat each other ; and foolish crystals getting in the way of wise ones ;
and impatient crystals spoiling the plans of
patient ones, irreparably ; just as things go
on in the world. And sometimes you may
see hypocritical crystals taking the shape of
others, though they are nothing like in their
minds ; and vampire crystals eating out the
hearts of others ; and hermit-crab crystals
living in the shells of others ; and parasite
crystals living on the means of others ; and
courtier crystals glittering in attendance upon
others ; and all these, besides the two great
companies of war and peace, who ally themselves, resolutely to attack, or resolutely to
defend. And for the close, you see the
broad shadow and deadly force of inevitable
fate, above all this : you see the multitudes
of crystals whose time has come ; not a set
time, as with us, but yet a time, sooner or
later, when they all must give up their crystal ghosts :—when the strength by which
they grew and the breath given them to
breathe, pass away from them ; and they fail,
and are consumed, and vanish away ; and
another generation is brought to life, framed
out of their ashes.

MARY. It is very terrible. Is it not the

complete fulfillment, down into the **very**
dust, of that verse: "The whole creation
groaneth and travaileth in pain"?

L. I do not know that it is in pain, Mary:
at least, the evidence tends to show that
there is much more pleasure than pain, as
soon as sensation becomes possible.

LUCILLA. But then, surely, if we are told
that it is pain, it must be pain?

L. Yes; if we are told; and told in the
way you mean, Lucilla; but nothing is said
of the proportion to pleasure. Unmitigated
pain would kill any of us in a few hours:
pain equal to our pleasures would make us
loathe life; the word itself cannot be applied
to the lower conditions of matter in its or-
dinary sense. But wait till to-morrow to
ask me about this. To-morrow is to be kept
for questions and difficulties; let us keep to
the plain facts to-day. There is yet one
group of facts connected with this rending
of the rocks, which I especially want you
to notice. You know, when you have
mended a very old dress, quite meritoriously,
till it won't mend any more——

EGYPT (*interrupting*). Could not you sometimes take gentlemen's work to illustrate by?

L. Gentlemen's work is rarely so useful
as yours, Egypt; and when it is useful,
girls cannot easily understand it.

DORA. I am sure we should understand it
better than gentlemen understand about
sewing.

L. My dear. I hope I always speak modestly, and under correction, when I touch upon matters of the kind too high for me ; and besidès, I never intend to speak otherwise than respectfully of sewing ;— though you always seem to think I am laughing at you. In all seriousness, illustrations from sewing are those which Neith likes me best to use ; and which young ladies ought to like everybody to use. What do you think the beautiful word " wife " comes from ?

DORA (*tossing her head*). I don't think it is a particularly beautiful word.

L. Perhaps not. At your ages you may think " bride " sounds better ; but wife's the word for wear, depend upon it. It is the great word in which the English and Latin languages conquer the French and the Greek. I hope the French will some day get a word for it, yet, instead of their dreadful "femme." But what do you think it comes from ?

DORA. I never *did* think about it.

L. Nor you, Sibyl ?

SIBYL. No ; I thought it was Saxon, and stopped there.

L. Yes ; but the great good of Saxon words is, that they usually do mean something. Wife means " weaver." You have all the right to call yourselves little " housewives," when you sew neatly.

DORA. But I don't think we want to call ourselves " little housewives."

L. You must either be house-Wives, or
house-Moths ; remember that. In the deep
sense, you must either weave men's fort-
unes, and embroider them ; or feed upon,
and bring them to decay. You had better
let me keep my sewing illustration, and
help me out with it.

DORA. Well, we'll hear it, under protest.

L. You have heard it before ; but with
reference to other matters. When it is said,
" No man putteth a piece of new cloth on
an old garment, else it taketh from the old,"
does it not mean that the new piece tears
the old one away at the sewn edge?

DORA. Yes ; certainly.

L. And when you mend a decayed stuff
with strong thread, does not the whole
edge come away sometimes, when it tears
again ?

DORA. Yes ; and then it is of no use to
mend it any more.

L. Well, the rocks don't seem to think
that : but the same thing happens to them
continually. I told you they were full of
rents, or veins. Large masses of mountain
are sometimes as full of veins as your hand
is ; and of veins nearly as fine (only you
know a rock vein does not mean a tube, but
a crack or cleft). Now these clefts are
mended, usually, with the strongest material the rock can find ; and often literally
with threads ; for the gradually opening rent
seems to draw the substance it is filled with

into fibers, which cross from one side of it to the other, and are partly crystalline ; so that when the crystals become distinct, the fissure has often exactly the look of a tear, brought together with strong cross stitches. Now when this is completely done, and all has been fastened and made firm, perhaps some new change of temperature may occur and the rock begin to contract again. Then the old vein must open wider ; or else another open elsewhere. If the old vein widen, it *may* do so at its center; but it constantly happens, with well filled veins, that the cross stitches are too strong to break ; the walls of the vein, instead, are torn away by them : and another little supplementary vein—often three or four successively—will be thus formed at the side of the first.

MARY. That is really very much like our work. But what do the mountains use to sew with?

L. Quartz, whenever they can get it : pure limestones are obliged to be content with carbonate of lime ; but most mixed rocks can find some quartz for themselves. Here is a piece of black slate from the Buet : it looks merely like dry dark mud ; you could not think there was any quartz in it ; but, you see, its rents are all stitched together with beautiful white thread, which is the purest quartz, so close drawn that you can break it like flint, in the mass ; but, where it has been

exposed to the weather, the fine fibrous structure is shown : and, more than that, you see
the threads have been all twisted and pulled
aside, this way and the other, by the warp-
ings and shifting of the sides of the vein as
it widened.

MARY. It is wonderful ! But is that going
on still ? Are the mountains being torn and
sewn together again at this moment?

L. Yes, certainly, my dear : but I think,
just as certainly (though geologists differ
on this matter), not with the violence, or
on the scale, of their ancient ruin and renewal.

All things seem to be tending towards a
condition of at least temporary rest ; and
that groaning and travailing of the creation,
as, assuredly, not wholly in pain, is not, in
the full sense, "until now."

MARY. I want so much to ask you about
that !

SIBYL. Yes ; and we all want to ask you
about a great many other things besides.

L. It seems to me that you have got quite
as many new ideas as are good for any of
you at present : and I should not like to
burden you with more ; but I must see that
those you have are clear, if I can make them
so ; so we will have one more talk, for answer
of questions, mainly. Think over all the
ground, and make your difficulties thoroughly
presentable. Then we'll see what we can
make of them.

Dora. They shall all be dresed in their very best ; and curtsey as they come in.

L. No, no, Dora ; no curtseys, if you please. I had enough of them the day you all took a fit of reverence, and curtsied me out of the room.

Dora. But, you know, we cured ourselves of the fault, at once, by that fit. We have never been the least respectful since. And the difficulties will only curtsey themselves out of the room, I hope ;—come in at one door—vanish at the other.

L. What a pleasant world it would be, if all its difficulties were taught to behave so ! However, one can generally made something, or (better still) nothing, or at least less, of them, if they thoroughly know their own minds ; and your difficulties—I must say that for you, children,—generally do know their own minds, as you do yourselves.

Dora. That is very kindly said for us. Some people would not allow so much as that girls had any minds to know.

L. They will at least admit that you have minds to change, Dora.

Mary. You might have left us the last speech, without a retouch. But we'll put our little minds, such as they are, in the best trim we can, for to-morrow.

LECTURE 10.

THE CRYSTAL REST.

LECTURE X.

THE CRYSTAL REST.

Evening. The fireside. L.'s arm-chair in the comfortable corner.

L. (*perceiving various arrangements being made of footstool, cushion, screen, and the like*). Yes, yes, it's all very fine! and I am to sit here to be asked questions till supper-time, am I?

DORA. I don't think you can have any supper to-night:—we've got so much to ask.

LILY. Oh, Miss Dora! We can fetch it him here, you know, so nicely!

L. Yes, Lily, that will be pleasant, with competitive examination going on over one's plate: the competition being among the examiners. Really, now that I know what teasing things girls are, I don't so much wonder that people used to put up patiently with the dragons who took *them* for supper. But I can't help myself, I suppose;—no thanks to St. George. Ask away, children, and I'll answer as civilly as may be.

DORA. We don't so much care about being answered civilly, as about not being asked things back again.

L. "Ayez seulement la patience que je le parle." There shall be no requitals.

DORA. Well, then, first of all—What shall we ask first, Mary ?

MARY. It does not matter. I think all the questions come into one, at last, nearly.

DORA. You know, you always talk as if the crystals were alive ; and we never understand how much you are in play, and how much in earnest. That's the first thing.

L. Neither do I understand, myself, my dear, how much I am in earnest. The stones puzzle me as much as I puzzle you. They look as if they were alive, and make me speak as if they were ; and I do not in the least know how much truth there is in the appearance. I'm not to ask things back again to-night, but all questions of this sort lead necessarily to the one main question, which we asked, before, in vain, "What is it to be alive?"

DORA. Yes ; but we want to come back to that : for we've been reading scientific books about the "conservation of forces," and it seems all so grand, and wonderful ; and the experiments are so pretty ; and I suppose it must be all right : but then the books never speak as if there were any such thing as "life."

L. They mostly omit that part of the subject, certainly, Dora ; but they are beautifully right as far as they go ; and life is not a convenient element to deal with. They seem to have been getting some of it into and out of bottles, in their "ozone" and "antizone" lately ; but they still know little of it : and, certainly, I know less.

DORA. You promised not to be provoking, to-night.

L. Wait a minute. Though, quite truly, I know less of the secrets of life than the philosophers do ; I yet know one corner of ground on which we artists can stand, literally as "Life Guards" at bay, as steadily as the Guards at Inkermann ; however hard the philosophers push. And you may stand with us, if once you learn to draw nicely.

DORA. I'm sure we are all trying ! but tell us where we may stand.

L. You may always stand by Form, against Force. To a painter, the essential character of anything is the form of it, and the philosophers cannot touch that. They come and tell you, for instance, that there is as much heat, or motion, or calorific energy (or whatever else they like to call it), in a tea-kettle as in a Gier-eagle. Very good ; that is so ; and it is very interesting. It requires just as much heat as will boil the kettle, to take the Gier-eagle up to his nest ; and as much more to bring him down again on a hare or a partridge. But we painters, acknowledging the equality and similarity of the kettle and the bird in all scientific respects, attach, for our part, our principal interest to the difference in their forms. For

us, the primarily cognizable facts, in the **two**
things, are, that the kettle has a spout, and
the eagle a beak ; the one a lid on its back,
the other a pair of wings ;—not to speak of
the distinction also of volition, which the
philosophers may properly call merely a
form, or mode of force ;—but then, to an
artist, the form, or mode, is the gist of the
business. The kettle chooses to sit still on
the hob ; the eagle to recline on the air. It
is the fact of the choice, not the equal degree
of temperature in the fulfillment of it, which
appears to us the more interesting circum-
stance ;—though the other is very interesting
too. Exceedingly so ! Don't laugh, chil·
dren ; the philosophers have been doing
quite splendid work lately, in their own
way : especially, the transformation of force
into light is a great piece of systematized
discovery ; and this notion about the sun's
being supplied with his flame by ceaseless
meteoric hail is grand, and looks very likely
to be true. Of course, it is only the old gun-
lock,—flint and steel,—on a large scale:
but the order and majesty of it are sublime.
Still, we sculptors and painters care little
about it. "It is very fine," we say, "and
very useful, this knocking the light out of
the sun, or into it, by an eternal cataract of
planets. But you may hail away, so, forever, and you will not knock out what we
can. Here is a bit of silver, not the size of
half-a-crown, on which, with a single ham-

mer stroke, one of us, two thousand and odd years ago, hit out the head of the Apollo of Clazomenæ. It is merely a matter of form ; but if any of you philosophers, with your whole planetary system to hammer with, can hit out such another bit of silver as this, —we will take off our hats to you. For the present, we keep them on."

MARY. Yes, I understand ; and that is nice ; but I don't think we shall any of us like having only form to depend upon.

L. It was not neglected in the making of Eve, my dear.

MARY. It does not seem to separate us from the dust of the ground. It is that breathing of the life which we want to understand.

L. So you should : but hold fast to the form, and defend that first, as distinguished from the mere transition of forces. Discern the molding hand of the potter commanding the clay, from his merely beating foot, as it turns the wheel. If you can find incense, in the vase, afterwards,—well : but it is curious how far mere form will carry you ahead of the philosophers. For instance, with regard to the most interesting of all their modes of force—light ;—they never consider how far the existence of it depends on the putting of certain vitreous and nervous substances into the formal arrangement which we call an eye, The German philosophers began the attack, long

ago, on the other side, by telling us, there
was no such thing as light at all, unless we
chose to see it : now, German and English,
both, have reversed their engines, and insist that light would be exactly the same
light that it is, though nobody could ever
see it.   The fact being that the force must
be there, and the eyes there ; and "light"
means the effect of the one on the other ;—
and perhaps, also—(Plato saw farther into
that mystery than any one has since, that
I know of),—on something a little way
within the eyes ; but we may stand quite
safe, close behind the retina, and defy the
philosophers.

SIBYL. But I don't care so much about
defying the philosophers, if only one could
get a clear idea of life, or soul, for one's self.

L. Well, Sibyl, you used to know more
about it. in that cave of yours, than any of
us.   I was just going to ask you about inspiration, and the golden bough, and the
like : only I remembered I was not to ask
anything.   But, will not you, at least, tell
us whether the ideas of Life, as the power
of putting things together, or "making"
them ; and of Death, as the power of pushing things separate, or "unmaking" them,
may not be very simply held in balance
against each other?

SIBYL. No, I am not in my cave to-night ;
and cannot tell you anything.

L. I think they may.   Modern Philosophy

is a great separator; it is little more than the expansion of Molière's great sentence, "Il s'ensuit de là, que tout ce qu'il y a de beau est dans les dictionnaires; il n'y a que les mots qui sont transposés." But when you used to be in your cave, Sibyl, and to be inspired, there was (and there remains still in some small measure), beyond the merely formative and sustaining power, another, which we painters call "passion" —I don't know what the philosophers call it; we know it makes people red, or white; and therefore it must be something, itself; and perhaps it is the most truly "poetic" or "making" force of all, creating a world of its own out of a glance, or a sigh: and the want of passion is perhaps the truest death, or "unmaking" of everything;—even of stones. By the way, you were all reading about that ascent of the Aiguille Verte, the other day?

SIBYL. Because you had told us it was so difficult, you thought it could not be ascended.

L. Yes; I believed the Aiguille Verte would have held its own. But do you recollect what one of the climbers exclaimed, when he first felt sure of reaching the summit?

SIBYL. Yes, it was, "Oh, Aiguille Verte, vous êtes morte, vous êtes morte!"

L. That was true instinct. Real philosophic joy. Now can you at all fancy the

difference between that feeling of triumph
in a mountain's death; and the exultation
of your beloved poet, in its life—

" Quantus Athos, aut quantus Eryx, aut ipse coruscis
    Quum fremit ilicibus quantus, gaudetque nivali
    Vertice, se attollens pater Apenninus ad auras."

DORA. You must translate for us mere
housekeepers, please—whatever the cave-
keepers may know about it.

MARY. Will Dryden do?

L. No. Dryden is a far way worse than
nothing, and nobody will "do." You can't
translate it. But this is all you need know,
that the lines are full of a passionate sense
of the Apennines' fatherhood, or protecting
power over Italy; and of sympathy with
their joy in their snowy strength in heaven;
and with the same joy, shuddering through
all the leaves of their forests.

MARY. Yes, that is a difference indeed!
but then, you know, one can't help feeling
that it is fanciful. It is very delightful to
imagine the mountains to be alive; but
then,—*are* they alive?

L. It seems to me, on the whole, Mary,
that the feelings of the purest and most
mightily passioned human souls are likely
to be the truest. Not, indeed, if they do
not desire to know the truth, or blind themselves to it that they may please themselves
with passion; for then they are no longer

pure : but if, continually seeking and accepting the truth as far as it is discernible, they trust their Maker for the integrity of the instincts He has gifted them with, and rest in the sense of a higher truth which they cannot demonstrate, I think they will be most in the right, so.

DORA *and* JESSIE (*clapping their hands*). Then we really may believe that the mountains are living?

L. You may at least earnestly believe that the presence of the spirit which culminates in your own life, shows itself in dawning, wherever the dust of the earth begins to assume any orderly and lovely state. You will find it impossible to separate this idea of graduated manifestation from that of the vital power. Things are not either wholly alive, or wholly dead. They are less or more alive. Take the nearest, most easily examined instance—the life of a flower. Notice what a different degree and kind of life there is in the calyx and the corolla. The calyx is nothing but the swaddling clothes of the flower ; the child-blossom is bound up in it, hand and foot ; guarded in it, restrained by it, till the time of birth. The shell is hardly more subordinate to the germ in the egg, than the calyx to the blossom. It bursts at last ; but it never lives as the corolla does. It may fall at the moment its task is fulfilled, as in the poppy ; or whether gradually, as in the buttercup ;

or persist in a ligneous apathy, after the
flower is dead, as in the rose ; or harmonize
itself so as to share in the aspect of the real
flower, as in the lily ; but it never shares in
the corolla's bright passion of life.   And the
gradations which thus exist between the
different members of organic creatures, exist
no less between the different ranges of or-
ganism.   We know no higher or more en-
ergetic life than our own ; but there seems
to me this great good in the idea of gradation of life—it admits the idea of a life above
us, in other creatures, as much nobler than
ours, as ours is nobler than that of the dust.

MARY. I am glad you have said that ; for
I know Violet and Lucilla and May want
to ask you something ; indeed, we all do ;
only you frightened Violet so about the ant-
hill, that she can't say a word ; and May is
afraid of your teasing her too : but I know
they are wondering why you are always
telling them about heathen gods and god-
desses, as if you half believed in them ;
and you represent them as good ; and then
we see there is really a kind of truth in the
stories about them ; and we are all puzzled :
and, in this, we cannot even make our difficulty quite clear to ourselves ;—it would be
such a long confused question, if we could
ask you all we should like to know.

L. Nor is it any wonder, Mary ; for this
is indeed the longest, and the most wildly
confused question that reason can deal with ;

but I will try to give you, quickly, a few
clear ideas about the heathen gods, which
you may follow out afterwards, as your
knowledge increases.

Every heathen conception of deity, in
which you are likely to be interested, has
three distinct characters :—

I. It has a physical character. It represents some of the great powers or objects
of nature—sun or moon, or heaven, or the
winds, or the sea. And the fables first related about each deity represent, figuratively,
the action or the natural power which it
represents ; such as the rising and setting of
the sun, the tides of the sea, and so on.

II. It has an ethical character, and represents, in its history, the moral dealings of
God with man. Thus Apollo is first, physically, the sun contending with darkness ;
but morally, the power of divine life contending with corruption. Athena is, physically, the air ; morally, the breathing of the
divine spirit of wisdom. Neptune is, physically, the sea ; morally, the supreme power
of agitating passion ; and so on.

III. It has, at last, a personal character ;
and is realized in the minds of its wor-
shipers as a living spirit, with whom men
may speak face to face, as a man speaks to
his friend.

Now it is impossible to define exactly,
how far, at any period of a national religion,
these three ideas are mingled ; or how far

one prevails over the other. Each inquirer
usually takes up one of these ideas, and
pursues it, to the exclusion of the others;
no impartial effort seems to have been made
to discern the real state of the heathen imagination in its successive phases. For the
question is not at all what a mythological
figure meant in its origin; but what it became in each subsequent mental development of the nation inheriting the thought.
Exactly in proportion to the mental and
moral insight of any race, its mythological
figures mean more to it, and become more
real. An early and savage race means
nothing more (because it has nothing more
to mean) by its Apollo, than the sun; while
a cultivated Greek means every operation
of divine intellect and justice. The Neith,
of Egypt, meant, physically, little more
than the blue of the air; but the Greek, in
a climate of alternate storm and calm, represented the wild fringes of the storm-cloud
by the serpents of her ægis; and the lightning and cold of the highest thunder-clouds,
by the Gorgon on her shield : while morally,
the same types represented to him the mystery and changeful terror of knowledge, as
her spear and helm its ruling and defensive
power. And no study can be more interesting, or more useful to you, than that of the
different meanings which have been created
by great nations, and great poets, out of
mythological figures given them, at first, in

utter simplicity. But when we approach
them in their third, or personal, character
(and, for its power over the whole national
mind, this is far the leading one), we are
met at once by questions which may well
put all of you at pause. Were they idly
imagined to be real beings? and did they so
usurp the place of the true God? Or were
they actually real beings,—evil spirits,—
leading men away from the true God? Or
is it conceivable that they might have been
real beings,—good spirits,—entrusted with
some message from the true God? These
were the questions you wanted to ask; were
they not, Lucilla?

LUCILLA. Yes, indeed.

L. Well, Lucilla, the answer will much
depend upon the clearness of your faith in
the personality of the spirits which are described in the book of your own religion;
—their personality, observe, as distinguished
from merely symbolical visions. For instance, when Jeremiah has the vision of the
seething pot with its mouth to the north,
you know that this which he sees is not a
real thing; but merely a significant dream.
Also, when Zechariah sees the speckled
horses among the myrtle-trees in the bottom,
you still may suppose the vision symbolical;
—you do not think of them as real spirits,
like Pegasus, seen in the form of horses.
But when you are told of the four riders in
the Apocalypse, a distinct sense of person-

ality begins to force itself upon you. And
though you might, in a dull temper, think
that (for one instance of all) the fourth rider
on the pale horse was merely a symbol of
the power of death,—in your stronger and
more earnest moods you will rather conceive of him as a real and living angel.
And when you look back from the vision of
the Apocalypse to the account of the destruction of the Egyptian first-born, and of
the army of Sennacherib, and again to
David's vision at the threshing floor of
Araunah, the idea of personality in this
death-angel becomes entirely defined, just as
in the appearance of the angels to Abraham,
Manoah, or Mary.

Now, when you have once consented to
this idea of a personal spirit, must not the
question instantly follow : "Does this spirit
exercise its functions towards one race of
men only, or towards all men? Was it an
angel of death to the Jew only, or to the
Gentile also?" You find a certain Divine
agency made visible to a King of Israel, as
an armed angel, executing vengeance, of
which one special purpose was to lower his
kingly pride. You find another (or perhaps
the same) agency, made visible to a Christian prophet as an angel standing in the sun,
calling to the birds that fly under heaven to
come, that they may eat the flesh of kings.
Is there anything impious in the thought
that the same agency might have been ex-

pressed to a Greek king, or Greek seer, by similar visions?—that this figure standing in the sun, and armed with the sword, or the bow (whose arrows were drunk with blood), and exercising especially its power in the humiliation of the proud, might, at first, have been called only "Destroyer," and afterwards, as the light, or sun, of justice, was recognized in the chastisement, called also "Physician" or "Healer"? If you feel hesitation in admitting the possibility of such a manifestation, I believe you will find it is caused, partly indeed by such trivial things as the difference to your ear between Greek and English terms; but, far more, by uncertainty in your own mind respecting the nature and truth of the visions spoken of in the Bible. Have any of you intently examined the nature of your belief in them? You, for instance, Lucilla, who think often, and seriously, of such things?

LUCILLA. No; I never could tell what to believe about them. I know they must be true in some way or other; and I like reading about them.

L. Yes; and I like reading about them too, Lucilla; as I like reading other grand poetry. But, surely, we ought both to do more than like it? Will God be satisfied with us, think you, if we read His words, merely for the sake of an entirely meaningless poetical sensation?

LUCILLA. But do not the people who give

themselves to seek out the meaning of these things, often get very strange, and extravagant?

L. More than that, Lucilla. They often go mad. That abandonment of the mind to religious theory, or contemplation, is the very thing I have been pleading with you against. I never said you should set yourself to discover the meanings : but you should take careful pains to understand them, so far as they *are* clear; and you should always accurately ascertain the state of your mind about them. I want you never to read merely for the pleasure of fancy ; still less as a formal religious duty (else you might as well take to repeating Paters at once; for it is surely wiser to repeat one thing we understand, than read a thousand which we cannot). Either, therefore, acknowledge the passage to be, for the present, unintelligible to you; or else determine the sense in which you at present receive them; or, at all events, the different senses between which you clearly see that you must choose. Make either your belief or your difficulty definite ; but do' not go on, all through your life, believing nothing intelligently, and yet supposing that your having read the words of a divine book must give you the right to despise every religion but your own. I assure you, strange as it may seem, our scorn of Greek tradition depends, not on our belief, but our disbelief, of our own traditions.

We have, as yet, no sufficient clue to the meaning of either ; but you will always find that, in proportion to the earnestness of our own faith, its tendency to accept a spiritual personality increases : and that the most vital and beautiful Christian temper rests joyfully in its conviction of the multitudinous ministry of living angels, infinitely varied in rank and power. You all know one expression of the purest and happiest form of such faith, as it exists in modern times, in Richter's lovely illustrations of the Lord's Prayer. The real and living death-angel, girt as a pilgrim for journey, and softly crowned with flowers, beckons at the dying mother's door ; child angels sit talking face to face with mortal children, among the flowers ;—hold them by their little coats, lest they fall on the stairs ; whisper dreams of heaven to them, leaning over their pillows ; carry the sound of the church bells for them far through the air ; and even descending lower in service, fill little cups with honey, to hold out to the weary bee. By the way, Lily, did you tell the other children that story about your little sister, and Alice, and the sea?

LILY. I told it to Alice, and to Miss Dora. I don't think I did to anybody else. I thought it wasn't worth.

L. We shall think it worth a great deal now, Lily, if you will tell it us. How old is Dotty, again? I forget.

LILY. She is not quite three ; but she has such odd little old ways, sometimes.

L. And she was very fond of Alice ?

LILY. Yes ; Alice was so good to her always !

L. And so when Alice went away ?

LILY. Oh, it was nothing, you know, to tell about ; only it was strange at the time.

L. Well ; but I want you to tell it.

LILY. The morning after Alice had gone, Dotty was very sad and restless when she got up ; and went about, looking into all the corners, as if she could find Alice in them, and at last she came to me, and said, "Is Alie gone over the great sea?" And I said, "Yes, she is gone over the great deep sea, but she will come back again some day." Then Dotty looked round the room; and I had just poured some water out into the basin ; and Dotty ran to it, and got up on a chair, and dashed her hands through the water, again and again ; and cried, " Oh, deep, deep sea ! send little Alie back to me."

L. Isn't that pretty, children ? There's a dear little heathen for you ! The whole heart of Greek mythology is in that ; the idea of a personal being in the elemental power ; —of its being moved by prayer ;—and of its presence everywhere, making the broken diffusion of the element sacred.

Now, remember, the measure in which we may permit ourselves to think of this trusted and adored personality, in Greek, or in any

other, mythology, as conceivably a shadow
of truth, will depend on the degree in which
we hold the Greeks, or other great nations,
equal, or inferior, in privilege and character,
to the Jews, or to ourselves. If we believe
that the great Father would use the imagination of the Jew as an instrument by which
to exalt and lead him ; but the imagination of
the Greek only to degrade and mislead him :
if we can suppose that real angels were sent
to minister to the Jews and to punish them ;
but no angels, or only mocking spectra of
angels, or even devils in the shapes of angels, to lead Lycurgus and Leonidas from
desolate cradle to hopeless grave :—and if
we can think that it was only the influence
of specters, or the teaching of demons,
which issued in the making of mothers like
Cornelia, and of sons like Cleobis and Bito,
we may, of course, reject the heathen Mythology in our privileged scorn ; but, at least,
we are bound to examine strictly by what
faults of our own it has come to pass, that
the ministry of real angels among ourselves
is occasionally so ineffectual as to end in the
production of Cornelias who entrust their
child-jewels to Charlotte Winsors for the better keeping of them ; and of sons like that
one who, the other day, in France, beat his
mother to death with a stick ; and was
brought in by the jury, "guilty, with ex-
tenuating circumstances."

May. Was that really possible.

L. Yes, my dear. I am not sure that I can lay my hand on the reference to it (and I should not have said "the other day,"— it was a year or two ago), but you may depend on the fact; and I could give you many like it, if I chose. There was a murder done in Russia, very lately, on a traveler. The murderess's little daughter was in the way, and found it out, somehow. Her mother killed her, too, and put her into the oven. There is a peculiar horror about the relations between parent and child, which are being now brought about by our variously degraded forms of European white slavery. Here *is* one reference, I see, in my notes on that story of Cleobis and Bito ; though I suppose I marked this chiefly for its quaintness and the beautifully Christian names of the sons ; but it is a good instance of the power of the King of the Valley of Diamonds * among us.

In "Galignani," of July 21–22, 1862, is reported a trial of a farmer's son in the department of the Yonne. The father, two years ago, at Malay le Grand, gave up his property to his two sons, on condition of being maintained by them. Simon fulfilled his agreement, but Pierre would not. The tribunal of Sens condemns Pierre to pay eighty-four francs a year to his father. Pierre replies, "he would rather die than

* Note vi.

pay it." Actually, returning home, he throws himself into the river, and the body is not found till next day.

MARY. But—but—I can't tell what you would have us think. Do you seriously mean that the Greeks were better than we are ; and that their gods were real angels ?

L. No, my dear. I mean only that we know, in reality, less than nothing of the dealings of our Maker with our fellow-men ; and can only reason or conjecture safely about them, when we have sincerely humble thoughts of ourselves and our creeds.

We owe to the Greeks every noble discipline in literature, every radical principle of art ; and every form of convenient beauty in our household furniture and daily occupations of life. We are unable, ourselves, to make rational use of half that we have received from them : and, of our own, we have nothing but discoveries in science, and fine mechanical adaptations of the discovered physical powers. On the other hand, the vice existing among certain classes, both of the rich and poor, in London, Paris, and Vienna, could have been conceived by a Spartan or Roman of the heroic ages only as possible in a Tartarus, where fiends were employed to teach, but not to punish, crime. It little becomes us to speak contemptuously of the religion of races to whom we stand in such relations ; nor do I think any man of modesty or thoughtfulness will ever speak

so of any religion, in which God has allowed
one good man to die, trusting.

The more readily we admit the possibility
of our own cherished convictions being
mixed with error, the more vital and helpful
whatever is right in them will become : and
no error is so conclusively fatal as the idea
that God will not allow *us* to err, though
He has allowed all other men to do so.
There may be doubt of the meaning of other
visions, but there is none respecting that of
the dream of St. Peter ; and you may trust
the Rock of the Church's Foundation for true
interpreting, when he learned from it that,
"in every nation, he that feareth God and
worketh righteousness, is accepted with
Him." See that you understand what that
righteousness means ; and set hand to it
stoutly : you will always measure your neighbors' creed kindly, in proportion to the sub-
stantial fruits of your own. Do not think
you will ever get harm by striving to enter
into the faith of others, and to sympathize,
in imagination, with the guiding principles
of their lives. So only can you justly love
them, or pity them, or praise. By the gracious efforts you will double, treble—nay, in-
definitely multiply, at once the pleasure, the
reverence, and the intelligence with which
you read : and, believe me, it is wiser and
holier, by the fire of your own faith, to kindle
the ashes of expired religions, than to let
your soul shiver and stumble among their

graves, through the gathering darkness, and communicable cold.

MARY (*after some pause*). We shall all like reading Greek history so much better after this ! but it has put everything else out of our heads that we wanted to ask.

L. I can tell you one of the things ; and I might take credit for generosity in telling you : but I have a personal reason—Lucilla's verse about the creation.

DORA. Oh, yes—yes ; and its "pain together, until now."

L. I call you back to that, because I must warn you against an old error of my own. Somewhere in the fourth volume of "Modern Painters," I said that the earth seemed to have passed through its highest state : and that, after ascending by a series of phases, culminating in its habitation by man, it seems to be now gradually becoming less fit for that habitation.

MARY. Yes, I remember.

L. I wrote those passages under a very bitter impression of the gradual perishing of beauty from the loveliest scenes which I knew in the physical world ;—not in any doubtful way, such as I might have attributed to loss of sensation in myself—but by violent and definite physical action ; such as the filling up of the Lac de Chêde by landslips from the Rochers des Fiz ;—the narrowing of the Lake Lucerne by the gaining delta of the stream of the Muotta-Thal,

which, in the course of years, will cut the
lake into two, as that of Brientz has been
divided from that of Thun ;—the steady
diminishing of the glaciers north of the Alps,
and still more, of the sheets of snow on their
southern slopes, which supply the refreshing
streams of Lombardy :—the equally steady
increase of deadly maremma round Pisa and
Venice ; and other such phenomena, quite
measurably traceable within the limits even
of short life, and unaccompanied, as it
seemed, by redeeming or compensatory
agencies. I am still under the same impression respecting the existing phenomena ;
but I feel more strongly, every day, that no
evidence to be collected within historical
periods can be accepted as any clew to the
great tendencies of geological change ; but
that the great laws which never fail, and to
which all change is subordinate, appear
such as to accomplish a gradual advance to
lovelier order, and more calmly, yet more
deeply, animated Rest. Nor has this conviction ever fastened itself upon me more
distinctly, than during my endeavor to trace
the laws which govern the lowly framework
of the dust. For, through all the phases of
its transition and dissolution, there seems to
be a continual effort to raise itself into a
higher state ; and a measured gain, through
the fierce revulsion and slow renewal of the
earth's frame, in beauty, and order, and per-
manence. The soft white sediments of the

sea draw themselves, in process of time,
into smooth knots of sphered symmetry;
burdened and strained under increase of
pressure, they pass into a nascent marble;
scorched by fervent heat, they brighten and
blanch into the snowy rock of Paros and
Carrara.   The dark drift of the inland river
or stagnant slime of inland pool and lake,
divides, or resolves itself as it dries, into
layers of its several elements; slowly puri-
fying each by the patient withdrawal of
it from the anarchy of the mass in which it
was mingled.   Contracted by increasing
drought, till it must shatter into fragments,
it infuses continually a finer ichor into the
opening veins, and finds in its weakness the
first rudiments of a perfect strength.   Rent
at last, rock from rock, nay, atom from
atom, and tormented in lambent fire, it
knits, through the fusion, the fibers of a per-
ennial endurance; and, during countless
subsequent centuries, declining, or, rather
let me say, rising, to repose, finishes the
infallible luster of its crystalline beauty,
under harmonies of law which are wholly
beneficent, because wholly inexorable.

(*The children seem pleased, but more inclined to think over these matters than
to talk.*)

L. (*after giving them a little time*). Mary, I
seldom ask you to read anything out of
books of mine; but there is a passage about
the Law of Help, which I want you to read

to the children now, because it is of no use merely to put it in other words for them. You know the place I mean, do not you ?

Mary. Yes (*presently finding it*); where shall I begin ?

L. Here ; but the elder ones had better look afterwards at the piece which comes just before this.

Mary (*reads*) :

" A pure or holy state of anything is that in which all its parts are helpful or consistent. The highest and first law of the universe, and the other name of life, is therefore ' help.' The other name of death is ' separation.' Government and co-operation are in all things, and eternally, the laws of life. Anarchy and competition, eternally, and in all things, the laws of death.

" Perhaps the best, though the most familiar, example we could take of the nature and power of consistence, will be that of the possible changes in the dust we tread on.

" Exclusive of animal decay, we can hardly arrive at a more absolute type of impurity, than the mud or slime of a damp, over-trodden path, in the outskirts of a manufacturing town. I do not say mud of the road, because that is mixed with animal refuse; but take merely an ounce or two of the blackest slime of a beaten footpath, on a rainy day, near a manufacturing town. That slime we shall find in most cases composed of clay (or brickdust, which is burnt clay), mixed with soot, a little sand and water. All these elements are at helpless war with each other, and destroy reciprocally each other's nature and power : competing and fighting for place at every tread of your foot ; sand squeezing out clay, and clay squeezing out water, and soot meddling everywhere, and defiling the whole. Let us suppose that this ounce of mud is left in perfect rest, and that its elements gather together, like to like, so that their atoms may get into the closest relations possible.

"Let the clay begin. Ridding itself of all foreign substance, it gradually becomes a white earth, already very beautiful, and fit, with help of congealing fire, to be made into finest porcelain, and painted on, and be kept in kings' palaces. But such artificial consistence is not its best. Leave it still quiet, to follow its own instinct of unity, and it becomes, not only white, but clear; not only clear, but hard; nor only clear and hard, but so set that it can deal with light in a wonderful way, and gather out of it the loveliest blue rays only, refusing the rest. We call it then a sapphire.

"Such being the consummation of the clay, we give similar permission of quiet to the sand. It also becomes, first, a white earth; then proceeds to grow clear and hard, and at last arranges itself in mysterious, infinitely fine parallel lines, which have the power of reflecting, not merely the blue rays, but the blue, green, purple, and red rays, in the greatest beauty in which they can be seen through any hard material whatsoever. We call it then an opal.

"In next order the soot sets to work. It cannot make itself white at first; but, instead of being discouraged, tries harder and harder; and comes out clear at last; and the hardest thing in the world; and for the blackness that it had, obtains in exchange the power of reflecting all the rays of the sun at once, in the vividest blaze that any solid thing can shoot. We call it then a diamond.

"Last of all, the water purifies, or unites itself; contented enough if it only reach the form of a dewdrop: but if we insist on its proceeding to a more perfect consistence, it crystallizes into the shape of a star. And, for the ounce of slime which we had by political economy of competition, we have, by political economy of co-operation, a sapphire, an opal, and a diamond, set in the midst of a star of snow.'

L. I have asked you to hear that, children, because, from all that we have seen in the

work and play of these past days, I would
have you gain at least one grave and endur-
ing thought. The seeming trouble,—the
unquestionable degradation,—of the elements of the physical earth, must passively
wait the appointed time of their repose, or
their restoration. It can only be brought
about for them by the agency of external
law. But if, indeed, there be a nobler life
in us than in these strangely moving atoms ;
—if, indeed, there is an eternal difference
between the fire which inhabits them, and
that which animates us,—it must be shown,
by each of us in his appointed place, not
merely in the patience, but in the activity
of our hope ; not merely by our desire, but
our labor, for the time when the Dust of the
generations of men shall be confirmed for
foundations of the gates of the city of God.
The human clay, now trampled and despised, will not be,—cannot be,—knit into
strength and light by accident or ordinances
of unassisted fate. By human cruelty and
iniquity it has been afflicted ;—by human
mercy and justice it must be raised : and, in
all fear or questioning of what is or is not,
the real message of creation, or of revela-
tion, you may assuredly find perfect peace,
if you are resolved to do that which your
Lord has plainly required,—and content
that He should indeed require no more of
you,—than to do Justice, to love Mercy,
and to walk humbly with Him.

NOTES.

NOTES.

NOTE I.

Page 32.

" That third pyramid of hers."

THROUGHOUT the dialogues, it must be observed that " Sibyl " is addressed (when in play) as having once been the Cumæan Sibyl; and " Egypt " as having been Queen Nitocris,—the Cinderella and " the greatest heroine and beauty " of Egyptian story. The Egyptians called her " Neith the Victorious " (Nitocris), and the Greeks " Face of the Rose " (Rhodope). Chaucer's beautiful conception of Cleopatra in the " Legend of Good Women," is much more founded on the traditions of her than on those of Cleopatra; and, especially in its close, modified by Herodotus's terrible story of the death of Nitocris, which, however, is mythologically nothing more than a part of the deep monotonous ancient dirge for the fulfillment of the earthly destiny of Beauty: " She cast herself into a chamber full of ashes."

I believe this Queen is now sufficiently ascertained to have either built, or increased to double its former size, the third pyramid of Gizeh: and the passage following in the text refers to an imaginary endeavor, by the Old Lecturer and the children together, to make out the description of that pyramid in the 167th page of the second volume of Bunsen's " Egypt's Place in Universal History "—ideal endeavor,—which ideally

terminates as the Old Lecturer's real endeavors to the
same end always have terminated. There are, however, valuable notes respecting Nitocris at page 210 of
the same volume: but the "Early Egyptian History
for the Young," by the author of " Sidney Gray " contains, in a pleasant form, as much information as young
readers will usually need.

NOTE II.

Page 33.

" Pyramid of Asychis."

THIS pyramid, in mythology, divides with the Tower
of Babel the shame, or vainglory, of being presumptu-
ously, and first among great edifices, built with "brick
for stone." This was the inscription on it, according
to Herodotus:

> " Despise me not, in comparing me with the
> pyramids of stone; for I have the pre-eminence
> over them, as far as Jupiter has pre-eminence over
> the gods. For, striking with staves into the pool,
> men gathered the clay which fastened itself to the
> staff, and kneaded bricks out of it, and so made
> me."

The word I have translated "kneaded" is literally
" drew ;" in the sense of drawing, for which the Latins
used " duco "; and thus gave us our " ductile " in speak-
ing of dead clay, and Duke, Doge, or leader, in speak-
ing of living clay. As the asserted pre-eminence of the
edifice is made, in this inscription, to rest merely on
the quantity of labor consumed in it, this pyramid is
considered, in the text, as the type, at once, of the base
building, and of the lost labor, of future ages, so far
at least as the spirits of measured and mechanical
effort deal with it; but Neith, exercising her power
upon it, makes it a type of the work of wise and inspired builders.

Note III.

Page 34.

" *The Greater Pthah.*"

IT is impossible, as yet, to define with distinctness the personal agencies of the Egyptian deities. They are continually associated in function, or hold derivative powers, or are related to each other in mysterious triads; uniting always symbolism of physical phenomena with real spiritual power. I have endeavored partly to explain this in the text of the tenth Lecture: here, it is only necessary for the reader to know that the Greater Pthah more or less represents the formative power of order and measurement: he always stands on a four-square pedestal, "the Egyptian cubit, metaphorically used as the hieroglyphic for truth;" his limbs are bound together, to signify fixed stability, as of a pillar; he has a measuring-rod in his hand; and at Philæ, is represented as holding an egg on a potter's wheel; but I do not know if this symbol occurs in older sculptures. His usual title is the "Lord of Truth." Others, very beautiful: "King of the Two Worlds, of Gracious Countenance," "Superintendent of the Great Abode," etc., are given by Mr. Birch in Arundale's "Gallery of Antiquities," which I suppose is the book of best authority easily accessible. For the full titles and utterance of the gods, Rosellini is as yet the only—and, I believe, still a very questionable —authority; Arundale's little book, excellent in the text, has this great defect, that its drawings give the statues invariably a ludicrous or ignoble character. Readers who have not access to the originals must be warned against this frequent fault in modern illustration (especially existing also in some of the painted casts of Gothic and Norman work at the Crystal Palace). It is not owing to any willful want of veracity: the plates in Arundale's book are laboriously faithful: but the expressions of both face and body in a figure

depend merely on emphasis of touch ; and, in barbaric
art, most draughtsmen emphasize what they plainly
see—the barbarism ; and miss conditions of nobleness,
which they must approach the monument in a different
temper before they will discover and draw with great
subtlety before they can express.

The character of the Lower Pthah, or perhaps I
ought rather to say, of Pthah in his lower office, is sufficiently explained in the text of the third Lecture ;
only the reader must be warned that the Egyptian
symbolism of him by the beetle was not a scornful
one ; it expressed only the idea of his presence in the
first elements of life. But it may not unjustly be used,
in another sense, by us, who have seen his power in
new development; and, even as it was, I cannot conceive that the Egyptians should have regarded their
beetle-headed image of him (Champollion, " Pantheon,"
pl. 12), without some occult scorn. It is the most pain-
ful of all their types of any beneficent power; and even
among those of evil influences, none can be compared
with it, except its opposite, the tortoise-headed demon
of indolence.

Pasht (p. 33, line 5) is connected with the Greek
Artemis, especially in her offices of judgment and
vengeance. She is usually lioness-headed ; sometimes
cat-headed; her attribute seeming often trivial or ludicrous unless their full meaning is known; but the in-
quiry is much too wide to be followed here. The cat
was sacred to her; or rather to the sun, and secondarily
to her. She is alluded to in the text because she is always the companion of Pthah (called " the beloved of
Pthah," it may be as Judgment, demanded and longed
for by Truth) ; and it may be well for young readers to
have this fixed in their minds, even by chance associa-
tion. There are more statues of Pasht in the British
Museum than of any other Egyptian deity; several of
them fine in workmanship; nearly all in dark stone,
which may be, presumably, to connect her, as the moon,
with the night ; and in her office of avenger, with
grief.

Thoth (p. 37, line 5) is the Recording Angel of

Judgment; and the Greek Hermes—Phre (line 9), is the Sun.

Neith is the Egyptian spirit of divine wisdom; and the Athena of the Greeks. No sufficient statement of her many attributes, still less of their meanings, can be shortly given; but this should be noted respecting the veiling of the Egyptian image of her by vulture wings —that as she is, physically, the goddess of the air, this bird, the most powerful creature of the air known to the Egyptians, naturally became her symbol. It had other significations; but certainly this, when in connection with Neith. As representing her, it was the most important sign, next to the winged sphere, in Egyptian sculpture; and, just as in Homer, Athena herself guides her heroes into battle, this symbol of wisdom, giving victory, floats over the heads of the Egyptian Kings. The Greeks, representing the goddess herself in human form, yet would not lose the power of the Egyptian symbol, and changed it into an angel of victory. First seen in loveliness on the early coins of Syracuse and Leontium, it gradually became the received sign of all conquest, and the so-called "Victory" of later times; which, little by little, loses its truth, and is accepted by the moderns only as a personification of victory itself, —not as an actual picture of the living Angel who led to victory. There is a wide difference between these two conceptions,—all the difference between insincere poetry, and sincere religion. This I have also endeavored farther to illustrate in the tenthLecture; there is, however, one part of Athena's character which it would have been irrelevant to dwell upon there; yet which I must not wholly leave unnoticed.

As the goddess of the air, she physically represents both its beneficent calm, and necessary tempest: other storm-deities (as Chrysaor and Æolus) being invested with a subordinate and more or less malignant function, which is exclusively their own, and is related to that of Athena as the power of Mars is related to hers in war. So also Virgil makes her able to wield the lightning herself, while Juno cannot, but must pray for the intervention of Æolus. She has precisely the correspondent

16

moral authority over calmness of mind, and just anger.
She soothes Achilles, as she incites Tydides; her physical power over the air being always hinted correlatively.
She grasps Achilles by his hair—as the wind would lift
it—softly,

> " It fanned his cheek, it raised his hair,
> Like a meadow gale in spring."

She does not merely turn the lance of Mars from Dio-
med; but seizes it in both her hands, and casts it aside,
with a sense of making it vain, like chaff in the wind;
—to the shout of Achilles, she adds her own voice of
storm in heaven—but in all cases the moral power is
still the principal one—most beautifully in that seizing
of Achilles by the hair, which was the talisman of his
life (because he had vowed it to the Sperchius if he re-
turned in safety), and which, in giving at Patroclus'
tomb, he, knowingly, yields up the hope of return to his
country, and signifies that he will die with his friend.
Achilles and Tydides are, above all other heroes, aided
by her in war, because their prevailing characters are
the desire of justice, united in both, with deep affections; and, in Achilles, with a passionate tenderness,
which is the real root of his passionate anger. Ulysses
is her favorite chiefly in her office as the goddess of
conduct and design.

NOTE IV.

Page 82.

" *Geometrical limitations.*"

It is difficult, without a tedious accuracy, or without
full illustration, to express the complete relations of
crystalline structure, which dispose minerals to take, at
different times, fibrous, massive, or foliated forms; and
I am afraid this chapter will be generally skipped by
the reader: yet the arrangement itself will be found
useful, if kept broadly in mind; and the transitions of

state are of the highest interest, if the subject is entered upon with any earnestness. It would have been vain to add to the scheme of this little volume any account of the geometrical forms of crystals : an available one, though still far too difficult and too copious, has been arranged by the Rev. Mr. Mitchell, for Orr's " Circle of the Sciences " ; and, I believe, the " nets " of crystals, which are therein given to be cut out with scissors and put prettily together, will be found more conquerable by young ladies than by other students. They should also, when an opportunity occurs, be shown, at any public library, the diagram of the crystallization of quartz referred to poles, at p. 8 of Cloizaux's " Manuel de Minéralogie " ; that they may know what work is ; and what the subject is.

With a view to more careful examination of the nascent states of silica, I have made no allusion in this volume to the influence of mere segregation, as connected with the crystalline power. It has only been recently, during the study of the breccias alluded to in page 186 that I have fully seen the extent to which this singular force often modifies rocks in which at first its influence might hardly have been suspected ; many apparent conglomerates being in reality formed chiefly by segregation, combined with mysterious brokenly-zoned structures, like those of some malachites. I hope some day to know more of these and several other mineral phenomena (especially of those connected with the relative sizes of crystals), which otherwise I should have endeavored to describe in this volume.

NOTE V.

Page 168.

" *St. Barbara.*"

I WOULD have given the legends of St. Barbara, and St. Thomas, if I had thought it always well for young readers to have everything at once told them which

they may wish to know. They will remember the
stories better after taking some trouble to find them ;
and the text is intelligible enough as it stands. The
idea of St. Barbara, as there given, is founded partly
on her legend in Peter de Natalibus, partly on the
beautiful photograph of Van Eyck's picture of her at
Antwerp ; which was some time since published at Lille.

Note VI.

Page 226.

" King of the Valley of Diamonds."

ISABEL interrupted the Lecturer here, and was briefly
bid to hold her tongue ; which gave rise to some talk,
apart, afterwards, between L. and Sibyl, of which a
word or two may be perhaps advisably set down.

SIBYL. We shall spoil Isabel, certainly, if we don't
mind ; I was glad you stopped her, and yet sorry ; for
she wanted so much to ask about the Valley of Diamonds again, and she has worked so hard at it, and
made it nearly all out by herself. She recollected
Elisha's throwing in the meal, which nobody else
did.

L. But what did she want to ask ?

SIBYL. About the mulberry trees and the serpents ;
we are all stopped by that. Won't you tell us what it
means ?

L. Now, Sibyl, I am sure you, who never explained
yourself, should be the last to expect others to do so.
I hate explaining myself.

SIBYL. And yet how often you complain of other
people for not saying what they meant. How I have
heard you growl over the three stone steps to purgatory : for instance !

L. Yes ; because Dante's meaning is worth getting
at ; but mine matters nothing ; at least, if ever I think
it is of any consequence, I speak it as clearly as may
be. But you may make anything you like of the ser-

pent forests. I could have helped you to find out what
they were, by giving a little more detail, but it would
have been tiresome.

SIBYL. It is much more tiresome not to find out.
Tell us, please, as Isabel says, because we feel so
stupid.

L. There is no stupidity; you could not possibly do
more than guess at anything so vague. But I think,
you, Sibyl, at least, might have recollected what first
dyed the mulberry?

SIBYL. So I did; but that helped little; I thought of
Dante's forest of suicides, too, but you would not simply
have borrowed that?

L. No. If I had had strength to use it, I should
have stolen it, to beat into another shape; not borrowed
it. But that idea of souls in trees is as old as the
world; or at least as the world of man. And I *did*
mean that there were souls in those dark branches;—
the souls of all those who had perished in misery
through the pursuit of riches, and that the river was
of their blood, gathering gradually, and flowing out of
the valley. Then I meant the serpents for the souls of
those who had lived carelessly and wantonly in their
riches; and who had all their sins forgiven by the
world, because they are rich : and therefore they have
seven crimson-crested heads, for the seven mortal sins;
of which they are proud : and these, and the memory
and report of them, are the chief causes of temptation
to others, as showing the pleasantness and absolving
power of riches; so that thus they are singing serpents.
And the worms are the souls of the common money-
getters and traffickers, who do nothing but eat and
spin: and who gain habitually by the distress or fool-
ishness of others (as you see the butchers have been
gaining out of the panic at the cattle plague, among
the poor),—so they are made to eat the dark leaves,
and spin, and perish.

SIBYL. And the souls of the great, cruel, rich people
who oppress the poor, and lend money to government
to make unjust war, where are they?

L. They change into the ice, I believe, and are knit

with the gold; and make the grave-dust of the valley. I believe so, at least, for no one ever sees those souls anywhere.

(SIBYL *ceases questioning.*)

ISABEL (*who has crept up to her side without any one seeing*). Oh, Sibyl, please ask him about the fireflies!

L. What, you there, mousie! No; I won't tell either Sibyl or you about the fireflies; nor a word more about anything else. You ought to be little fireflies yourselves, and find your way in twilight by your own wits.

ISABEL. But you said they burned, you know?

L. Yes; and you may be fireflies that way too, some of you, before long, though I did not mean that. Away with you, children. You have thought enough for to-day.

NOTE TO SECOND EDITION.

Sentence out of letter from May (who is staying with Isabel just now at Cassel), dated 15th June, 1877 :—

" I am reading the Ethics with a nice Irish girl who is staying here, and she's just as puzzled as I've always been about the fireflies, and we both want to know so much.—Please be a very nice old Lecturer, and tell us, won't you ? "

Well, May, you never were a vain girl; so could scarcely guess that I meant them for the light, unpursued vanities, which yet blind us, confused among the stars. One evening, as I came late into Siena, the fireflies were flying high on a stormy sirocco wind,—the stars themselves no brighter, and all their host seeming, at moments, to fade as the insects faded.

www.ingramcontent.com/pod-product-compliance
Lightning Source LLC
Chambersburg PA
CBHW020754250626
47155CB00003B/1071